D1391658

Royal Navy Ships' Badges

Royal Navy Ships' Badges

by
Peter C. Smith

*The photographs of the badges are reproduced by kind permission of the
National Maritime Museum, Greenwich*

A Balfour Book, printed and published by Photo Precision Ltd.,
St. Ives, Huntingdon, England.

ACKNOWLEDGEMENTS

The author would like to acknowledge the invaluable assistance given to him by the following: John Munday, Lieutenant David Lyon and Miss D. E. Williams, all of the National Maritime Museum, London; Walter J. Verco, C.V.O., Norroy and Ulster King of Arms, College of Heralds, London; Miss Belinda Loftus, Department of Art, Imperial War Museum, London; Rear Admiral P. N. Buckley, C.B., D.S.O., Naval Historical Branch, Warships Names Committee, London, and J. W. Plummer, Planning Department, H.M. Dockyard, Chatham.

BY THE SAME AUTHOR:

Destroyer Leader
Task Force 57
Pedestal
Stuka at War
Hard Lying
British Battle Cruisers
War in the Aegean (with Edwin Walker)
Heritage of the Sea

FIRST EDITION 1974

© Peter C. Smith

ISBN 0 85944 011 7

Contents

*The great lion figurehead
of the 3rd rate Hogue.
Such figureheads were
symbolic of the ship much
as the badges are today.*

The History of Warships' Names and the Origins of Naval Heraldry

The study of the ships' badges carried by all vessels of the Royal Navy will reward the reader with a fascinating insight into the whole spectrum of naval history and tradition. The custom of carrying an individual badge is a comparatively recent innovation but is a direct descendant of other and far older manifestations of heraldry in the Royal Navy.

Among the numerous inanimate artifacts which man has accumulated about himself the ship is one of the most ancient and is also the one which possesses in abundance individualistic characteristics closely resembling a living creature. Rudyard Kipling's classic little tale, *The ship that found herself,* describes perfectly the feeling of movement and life which make up whole sections of steel and machinery into something akin to life. How much more 'alive' then must have seemed the sailing ships of bygone ages, especially to the more unsophisticated and sentimental sailor of those times.

Little wonder then, that from time immemorial ships have been graced with names and are still today always referred to as 'she'. She, your ship, could be a hard mistress indeed in bad weather but a comfort and a mother as well. Over the centuries these names have become identified with stirring episodes and valorous deeds, thus gaining by association extra prestige and affection. And so, today, they provide the modern rating in his steel-enmeshed floating computer with a tenuous link with the wooden walls and hearts-of-oak of his famous forebears.

In the earliest days there was no established fighting fleet and names were general to all types of vessel, and were, more often than not, of a mystic or religious nature. In these frail little craft the crews, once at sea, were certainly in the hands of their Maker, thus we find *Jesus* of 1420, innumerable *Mary's* from 1350 onward and *Trinity* of 1414.

During the early 16th century ships began to be built specifically for combat and Henry VIII is well known for the laying of the firm foundations of a permanent fighting fleet. The royal influence on ships names therefore became prominent with names like *Sovereign, Regent* and the older *Queen* becoming identified with warships. The new-found spirit of combat and defiance at sea enhanced by the stirring deeds of Elizabethan mariners was also reflected with such aggressive names as *Dreadnought, Revenge* and *Victory.*

And so it continued, each new name soon added lustre to itself with combat and passed on the pride in the ship, and the service, to its successor. The Commonwealth saw the beginnings of organised fighting at sea with the famous Generals-at-Sea like

Monck conducting operations to a grand plan rather than an 'each ship for herself' basis. It was during this period that the naming of ships after victorious battles became popular, although with the Restoration these vessels were hastily renamed to eradicate all memories of royal defeats from the minds of the king's sailors.

The foundations of the British Empire were securely laid during the late 18th and early 19th centuries by British seapower which reached the pinnacle of its prestige with an unbroken series of victories over the French and Spanish culminating in Trafalgar. After this the period of 'Pax Britannica' continued for over a hundred years and Britain's colonial expansion continued behind the unchallenged shield of the Royal Navy. It was not until the turn of the century that the gauntlet was again thrown down by Kaiser Wilhelm's Germany. Already the greatest land power in the world, Germany sought to challenge Britain's long established predominance at sea also.

The British response was to build the mightiest fleet in her history and the names borne by the great battleships of that period, which ended with the surrender of the German High Seas Fleet in 1918, are among the most stirring to be found in any assembly of warships.

The enormous expansion of the fleets in both world wars far outstripped the supply of old established names and a special naming committee had to be set up to cope with the demand for fresh names for the ships large and small which poured out of the shipyards between 1914-18 and 1939-45. The names had to be both stirring and suitable, no mean task this for the sailor is a notorious humorist. When the naming of submarines was abandoned for a time during the Second World War some quite unique, but hardly acceptable, unofficial names were given before the Admiralty was forced to relent.

Even so many of these comparatively recent names have added their own distinctive aura in combat to the annals of the Royal Navy and have in their turn quickly become 'traditional'. A well-known example of this is the 'Tribal' class. Many of these names were introduced for a class of large destroyers built by 'Jackie' Fisher in 1909. Their exploits with the famed Dover Patrol during the Great War gave these 'new' names a proud record which was passed on in the late thirties to another large class of destroyer. Here we can see another association, that of a particular group of names becoming associated with a distinct type of warship. Thus the accepted cruiser names were those of counties and cities. To revert again to the 'Tribal's, the new destroyers, if

The figurehead of the Ajax *another 3rd rate ship-of-line showing the detail these figureheads displayed.*

8

anything, exceeded the fame of their predecessors, and names like *Cossack, Ashanti* and *Nubian* became household words during the war. Since then the 'Tribal' names have again been revived for a group of frigates, which are the modern equivalent of destroyers, thus perpetuating the tradition.

With the passing of the battleship and the large cruiser from the naval scene the old line-of-battle ships' names honoured for centuries have been passed on to the battleships of the 70's, the nuclear-powered submarines, and thus we now see in the fleet again the proud names of *Dreadnought, Valiant, Warspite* and *Renown.*

It can thus be seen how the continuity of a ship's name is a worthy part of the tradition of the Royal Navy. Naturally enough the sailor was to make more obvious manifestations of this pride in the decoration of the ships themselves. Thus we have the figureheads and finely carved embellishments to the sterns and bows of warships typified by the magnificent *Sovereign of the Seas* and the like. These often incorporated a representation of the ship's name in the figurehead and happily some good examples of these are still to be found.

With the passing of the age of sail the opportunity to perpetuate such visible affection for a ship was gradually lost. The strictly functional steel warships of the late 19th and early 20th-century presented more of a workmanlike than ornate appearance and the hitherto limited differences in superficial appearance anyway between warship and merchantman became more and more marked and obvious. True, the ship's name was still carried, usually in raised letters on the ship's stern and later, with the introduction of ships' nameplates, which still exist, mounted on the after superstructure, but this was rather a spartan inheritance from the ornate gilding of the earlier centuries. Attempts to enhance this limited field met with a varied response. For example in 1937 the new light cruiser *Southampton*, while serving with the Mediterranean Fleet, carried an immaculate name plaque which at night was lit up quite impressively. This provoked the following signal from the Rear-Admiral (Destroyers) at that time, James Somerville:

'As a shareholder in the Southern Railway I must protest at
what can only be called pilfering of one of the platform signs of
the station whose name your flagship bears'.

Also during this transition period the figurehead had been replaced by elaborate scroll work on the bows which often incorporated coats of arms, as of old, with the wreaths and embellishments carried round the sides of the bow. But again, as the design of warships became more and more practical, this decoration also gradually vanished. The direct line of descent from figurehead to modern day badge is represented by such ships as *Orion* and *Swiftsure* whose badges actually incorporated the design of the original figurehead.

During this period, 1860 to 1914, when these decorations were becoming more and more rare, ships began to use unofficial badges and crests for prestige purposes, usually boats badges but also on their notepaper and many very attractive designs appeared in this form. The decorating of the gun tampions also dates from this period and a later example of this is shown.

During the Great War an enormous number of new ships were built for the expanded fleet and the examples of ships badges dating from the period show that the designs were as varied as the number of the ships themselves. They still of course remained unofficial but it was towards the end of this era that the first steps were taken to standardise their appearance.

This came about through the work and diligent research of Major Charles ffoulkes, the former Master of the Tower Armouries and, later, a Director of the Imperial War Museum. Because of his former association he was approached by the Commanding Officer of the new destroyer H.M.S. *Tower*, which was then under construction and took her name from the Tower of London. Major ffoulkes produced a badge showing the White Tower and so impressed were naval circles and the shipbuilding industry that he was subsequently approached to design others for ships of the same class, *Tintagel* and *Tara*.

This led Major ffoulkes to research the whole question of the origins and production of ships' badges and, because it was felt that many of the designs produced erred on the side of frivolity and were not really in keeping with the tradition and continuity of the service, he offered to supply badges for H.M. ships and for them to be made official for recognition and prestige reasons. This offer was accepted by an enlightened Board in December 1918 and the Ships' Badges Committee was set up with Major ffoulkes, as the foremost expert, appointed as the Admiralty adviser on Heraldry.

Stern view of a model of the battle-cruiser Queen Mary *which shows how by the early twentieth century the decoration shown on the* Victory *(page 14) had been reduced to much simpler design.*

Their immediate conclusion was that in order to present a uniform aspect each type of warship would have its own distinctive shape of crest to which the badge would be affixed. Observations were made from a captured German submarine moored on the Thames at Westminster and the final decision was that in future battleships should have a circular shape, cruisers a pentagon, destroyers a shield shape, with a diamond shape for aircraft carriers, submarines and auxiliary craft.

So many ships were on the Navy List at this time that allocating suitable badges for them all proved a massive task involving much patient research. Once the designs were approved they were sent to Messrs. Martyns, the Palace Decorators, of Cheltenham, who produced the carvings. In the first year alone no less than 113 designs were approved and the carvings were placed on display at Gieves in Bond Street, London.

There were some quite unlooked for difficulties for, despite all attempts at providing suitable and apt names by the Ships Names Committee, typists slips and sailors humour sometimes combined to produce names that were hardly the most traditional. For example a typist slip changed the name of the destroyer *Stirling*, named after Stirling Castle, to *Sterling!* As an example of a name considered suitable but laughed out by the lower deck we have the sloop *Weston-super-Mare.* She was promptly dubbed, while building, *Aggie-on-horseback*, one Dame Agnes Weston being the patron of Naval hostelries. The Admiralty had perforce to change the sloop's name to *Weston.*

Often the unofficial badges reflected the same response. The old frigate *Simoom* was named after the hot dry wind of the Sahara and her badge showed a camel under a palm tree. On being told that this was hardly suitable the ship's captain and officers produced a variant showing the palm tree bent almost double under a wind of hurricane violence with coconuts being hurled about, with a very upset camel looking most uncomfortable.

The actual carving of the badges eventually passed into the skilled hands of Mr. H. L. Maschek who once worked for Martyns and who subsequently worked on his own for over thirty years, in Wembley, London. After he had carved them in yellow pine they were approved by the Admiralty Committee and then delivered to Chatham Dockyard. Here the carvings were made ready and were cast in brass at the Dockyard foundry. This very involved process no longer takes place however for with the march of time the foundry no longer exists.

Nowadays, and for years, the badges have been manufactured from epoxy resin and fibre glass in the patternmakers' shop where the badges were first made. All the original approved designs for ships' badges are held at the Dockyard and once registered, the official badge of any ship used for any purpose cannot be altered without permission of the Ships' Badges Committee. The ships, boats and tampion badges are always of the same design. With the passing of the traditional types of warship, battleship, cruiser, destroyer and now aircraft carrier, the new types of ships which bear the old names carry the shape of badge of their original predecessors. Thus the new nuclear-powered submarine *Warspite* carries the circular badge of the old battleship, while the new frigate *Amazon* has the shield type of its destroyer forbear of 1927. In the rare case of a name being allocated which has not had a previous badge then all such new badges are circular regardless of what type of ship is to carry it.

The gun tampion of the battleship Revenge which shows how the main features of the ship's badge were incorporated.

Major ffoulkes work continued for some seventeen years during which time he is credited with the design of no less than 556 ships badges. As there are at least 2,000 suitable names available to the Royal Navy, however, his work, although outstanding, was by no means exhaustive. His place as adviser on Heraldry on the Ships' Badges Committee was taken over by a representative from the College of Arms.

However it has never been the case, as has often been written, that the College of Arms then became solely responsible for the design of Ships' Badges. The misconception that the College is responsible arises from the fact that an Officer of

Arms of the College of Arms has always been appointed by the Admiralty as their adviser in these matters. In fact the actual initial design of the badge still rests on the Ships' Names Committee.

The ship itself can submit a design to which, if approved by the Committee, the College adds the correct heraldic description so that they are 'truly described'. For example the numerous 'Hunt' class destroyers of the Second World War all had their badges designed as adaptions of the emblems of the Hunts themselves which involved careful study by the College.

When the original approved designs for ships' badges are finished with they are filed in the Drawing Office at Chatham Dockyard as the sealed pattern. These are photographed and copies sent to the Admiralty and the ship, while the negatives are stored securely. The ships' staff can, if conforming to certain conditions, be allowed a rubber mould for the manufacture of badges, from a plaster compound, for presentation purposes.

All the badges illustrated in this book, being permanent exhibits, are copyright of the National Maritime Museum. Black and white prints of any ship's badge can be obtained from H.M. Dockyard, Chatham. They are also Crown Copyright and subject to certain 'Conditions of Sale'.

Ships badges remain today almost the only heraldic decoration for warships and with the passing of the gun as the principal weapon, tampions feature more and more rarely, while the casting of boats badges has almost ceased also. The Fleet Air Arm Squadrons of yesteryear each had their own distinctive badge as well but soon only those remaining on the helicopter units will remain. The Ships' badge however survives as a unique and colourful link with the past. Long may it remain so.

The nameplate of the destroyer Cavalier *shows the simpler design of the present day warship. (Copyright of the author).*

This bow view of the Cavalier *shows all the positions of the ship's badge on a modern man-of-war. Her badge and crest can be seen on her gun tampions, her bridge and on the covers of her radar arrays. (Copyright of the author).*

The following section, Part 1, illustrates examples of the Ships' Badges themselves with details of the histories of the vessels bearing the name. The ships' badges were mounted upon the crest which consists of the Naval Crown, flanked alternately by the sails and sterns views of galleons. Part 2 illustrates and describes in the same manner examples of the Boats' Badges. These were identical in all respects to the Ships' Badges save they did not feature the crest. They were affixed to the ships' small boats, gigs, whalers and the like, and were faithful reproductions of the main Ship's Badge, although of course much smaller.

Part One

Ships' Badges

H.M.S. Benbow

The name derives from Vice-Admiral John Benbow (1653-1702) a gallant naval officer who was killed in action against a superior French squadron in the West Indies.

The first ship to carry the name was a 3rd-rate built towards the end of the wars against the same enemy in 1813. She had a long but largely uneventful life, the only battle honour being recorded for her being that of Syria in 1840. She was laid up after this but not finally sold until 1894.

Long before the disposal of the first *Benbow* the second and most famous ship of the name was laid down. She was one of the 'Admiral' class battleships built between 1882 and 1888. This class was the first class of capital ships to be built to ensure some uniformity in design following many years of experiment. The 'Admirals' were the first British battleships to completely abandon any sort of sail power. Up to that time masts and spars had been a continuing feature despite the advances made in machinery. They also adopted the breech loading gun after long and detailed examination of the merits or otherwise of many types by the Naval and Military Ordnance Committee in 1881. However, whereas her four sister ships were equipped with four of the 67-ton 13.5-inch guns the *Benbow* herself mounted the colossal 110 ton 16.25 inch guns built at Elswick.

In fact the selection of this monster gun was only a second best choice, for with the call for accelerated building to improve the strength of the fleet at this time, a major factor in building times was the supply of the guns themselves. As Woolwich seemed unable to provide the necessary 13.5-inch guns fitted to her sisters the only alternative heavy gun was the 16.25-inch of Elswick.

These big guns were mounted in barbettes and for a considerable time in the late Victorian navy arguments had raged over the merits of this system over that of the turret. The barbette was a heavily armoured citadel in which the guns were mounted on a revolving platform. The disadvantages of this system were that the crews were completely exposed to gunfire and the elements. In the turret system the whole citadel was enclosed with the guns being laid and fired through sights and the whole mass revolved.

Eventually the barbette system prevailed being lighter in weight, an important consideration in warship design, which in turn enabled the guns themselves to be carried higher out of the water, with resulting better command of fire. With the advent of the quick firing gun these were fitted with hoods and this combination came over the years to be called *turrets* and the word barbette was only applied to the fixed base.

Because of their size she could only mount two of these mighty weapons but it was considered that the hitting power of these would prove decisive, although the rate of fire was much slower and the life of the gun was only 75 rounds. She was built on the Thames at Blackwall, being laid down in November 1882 and completed in June 1888 at a cost of some £764,022. In addition to her two 16.25-inch guns mounted fore and aft in single barbettes of 14-inch thickness, she carried ten 6-inch and twelve 6-pdr. guns and five torpedo tubes. She was 330 feet overall and displaced 10,600 tons. She had a crew of 524 and a speed of 17 knots and she proved an excellent sea boat in service.

Without a doubt it was the possession of two of the biggest guns in the fleet at the time that placed her in high favour with the public at large. She commissioned at Chatham for service with the Mediterranean fleet and remained on that station until 1891 before paying off into reserve at Chatham the year after. Here she was kept, being taken into service only for the summer manoeuvres of 1892-3 before going to Greenock as guard ship until 1904. She then went to reserve at Devonport until she was sold for scrap in July 1909.

Her successor was also a mighty battleship, being one of the *Iron Duke* class which were completed just before the outbreak of World War I. The *Iron Duke* herself became famed as Jellicoe's flagship with the Grand Fleet and the new *Benbow* served her war service with this mighty array of power.

The battleships of this class displaced some 25,000 tons and carried ten 13.5-inch guns in twin mountings, together with twelve 6-inch guns and four torpedo tubes. Up until this class the 'Dreadnoughts' of the British fleet had not mounted a larger calibre secondary armament than 4-inch guns because Fisher was determined to keep his battleships all big-gun vessels so that the shell splashes of the lighter calibre did not disturb the laying of the main guns, but advances in control and gunlaying had largely overcome this problem and the increasing size and power of the destroyer meant that the 6-inch gun firing shrapnel was the only really effective answer to a mass attack by torpedo-carrying craft in misty weather.

Benbow built by Beardmore, was completed in October 1912 at a cost of around £1,891,000 which, if compared with her predecessor of a quarter of a century earlier, gives some indication of the rising cost of shipbuilding.   She served throughout the war with the 4th Battle Squadron as the flagship first of Sir Douglas Gamble and then of Sir Doveton Sturdee and fought at Jutland without any casualties. Post-war, she went out to the Mediterranean from 1919 to 1926 and was involved in the Black Sea operations during the final stages of the Russian Revolution and its many complications in that area. Between 1926 and 1929 she served with the Atlantic Fleet and was not finally discarded until January 1931.

The name has not again been revived for a fighting ship although it was in use for the naval base at Trinidad between 1941 and 1947, appropriately enough in consideration of Vice-Admiral Benbow's final battle almost 240 years earlier.

H.M.S. Cavendish

The ship was named after Thomas Cavendish the great navigator who circumnavigated the globe in 1586 to 1588 and the badge itself is taken from the Cavendish arms. Her ship's motto was *Cavendo tutus,* Safe by taking care.

The first ship to be allocated this name was one of the very large cruisers built towards the end of the Great War all of which were named after famous seamen, her sisters being *Effingham, Raleigh* and *Frobisher.* Carrying 7.5-inch guns as originally designed they were completed too late for the war and did not finally join the fleet until the early 1920's. In the meantime, while they were still building, it had been decided to fit out the *Cavendish* herself as a seaplane carrier. As she would then have little or no resemblance to her sisters it was decided to rename her *Vindictive* after the famous old ship which took part in the blocking of Zeebrugge harbour in 1918.

The second *Cavendish* was a destroyer of the 11th Emergency Flotilla, built during the Second World War. She was to have been named *Sibyl* but in order to provide a class of destroyers all carrying the prefix 'Ca' she and her sisters were renamed. The 'Ca' class were standard wartime destroyers and had been evolved throughout the war on the basic hull and dimensions of the pre-war 'J' class boats, but with a much reduced main armament due to the difficulties of supply.

Cavendish was therefore armed with four single 4.5-inch dual-purpose guns as her main armament, and these were backed up with a powerful anti-aircraft defence which consisted of a twin 40mm bofors, and eight 20mm oerlikons. She was also armed with two quadruple sets of 21-inch torpedo tubes and could carry up to 70 depth-charges for anti-submarine work.

She had an overall length of 362¾ feet and a breadth of 35 feet 8 inches and a standard displacement of 1,710 tons. Her engines were the standard Parsons I.R. single reduction turbines developing a S.H.P. of 40,000 which gave them a legend speed of 35 knots. Her boilers were the Admiralty 3-drum type developing 300 lbs p.s.i. and she could carry around 500 tons of oil fuel.

Built by John Brown's shipyard, she was launched on 30th May 1944 and on completion she joined the 6th Destroyer Flotilla, Home Fleet, just in time for the closing stages of the war in Europe. A new type of propeller was tried out in *Cavendish* which proved most satisfactory.

She saw some limited service with the Home Fleet in home waters and off Norway during 1945 and also served in the Western Approaches for a time during which period some trouble was had with her torpedo tubes which required dockyard service to correct. Along with others of her flotilla she was earmarked to join the British Pacific Fleet for the final attacks on Japan, and was thus taken in hand for modification to enable her to operate in the Far East. On conclusion of these alterations she sailed for her new station but the Japanese surrender came before she joined that theatre of operations.

With the end of the war the ships served briefly in the Far East and in the Indian Ocean but by the end of 1946 all had returned to their home ports to pay off and go into reserve. Here their vital armaments and other exposed equipment was preserved in plastic cocoons and with only an occasional inspection to check on their condition *Cavendish* and her sisters remained thus for almost ten years.

During this long period of inactivity the equipment and design, and in many cases even the function, of the destroyer had been questioned and put to much discussion. Many of *Cavendish's* near sisters of the 'R' to 'V' classes, although quite modern ships at the time, had been reduced to frigates. This involved the removal of almost all of their aggressive armament, guns and torpedo tubes, and the stripping down of their upperworks. They were then rebuilt to give a much greater seaworthiness and fitted out with a reduced gun armament and greatly increased anti-submarine potential. As such they were no longer destroyers but merely fast escorts for convoy work, although they still retained their destroyer engines which meant that for a considerable period they were the only escorts capable of thirty knots in the post-war fleet. As in many instances these refits proved expensive and in the post-war world of defence economies many of the destroyer conversions carried out were on a smaller scale, only the armament being reduced without the rebuilding. A great deal of scrapping of under-age ships had also taken place until by 1955 the Royal Navy was a pale shadow of its former might.

It was then that the shortage of fast destroyers began to be noticed and it was realised that in the eight ships of the 'Ca' class the Navy had a flotilla of fast ships which had seen practically no sea service at all. They were therefore selected to be brought forward into service again as almost new ships, but as each one was selected a refit was given to bring her more up to date with the requirements of the 1950's.

Cavendish commenced her modernisation in January 1954 when her bridge was rebuilt and a new Mark VI director was installed with whip aerials. 'X' 4.5 inch gun was landed and in its place two of the new anti-submarine mortars, Squids, were installed. As such she sailed to join the 8th Destroyer Squadron in the Far East. Here she continued to serve at intervals, with refits between each commission, until the mid-1960's with periods on the Home Fleet and Mediterranean stations. By this time however her hull was over twenty years old, well past the life span of a destroyer, and she was broken up. All her sisters were due to follow her to the same end, but happily *Cavalier*, the last destroyer in full seagoing commission, was selected to be saved for the nation. Thus it is that at least one of *Cavendish's* sisters survives to this day, the last ship fully entitled to carry the proud name of destroyer. The name *Cavendish* itself however has passed out of the Navy.

H.M.S. Glowworm

The name is a comparatively recent one in the history of the Royal Navy, originating during the First World War. But, recent though the name may be, it has a high place in the annals of gallantry and self-sacrifice in the service. The badge shown is that of a gunboat built in 1915 but it was the second vessel of that name which brought lustre to it.

She was a 1,360 ton destroyer of the *Gallant* class, launched from the yard of Thornycroft's at Woolston in 1935. The British destroyers of this period were trim, graceful and seaworthy little craft which carried four 4.7-inch guns and two banks of quadruple 21-inch torpedo tubes. *Glowworm* was, however, the first destroyer to carry the new quintuple mounting and thus had ten torpedoes against the eight of her sister ships.

The adoption of the quintuple torpedo mounting was a reflection on the Staff requirements of the time. When *Glowworm* was laid down the flotillas were still training hard in the perfection of mass night torpedo attacks against an enemy battle-line. It has been argued since that the need for such training had long passed for no potential enemy had sufficient battleships to form a traditional line. This argument however ignored two things. Firstly, there were at least two fleets, Japan and the United States, which had ten or more battleships. War against America was termed unthinkable, but war against Japan was considered quite likely, therefore fleet attacks were a basic requirement. It also followed that the training received by all members of the destroyer's crew in such high speed night attacks brought them up to a high pitch of efficiency and there was no hesitation about handling their frail craft at night. Such readiness equipped them for *any* emergency, not just a classic torpedo attack and was therefore invaluable. Lack of such training was reflected in the poor handling of such fleets as the Italian and resulted in the battle of Matapan. The quintuple torpedo mounting was therefore subsequently adopted by several destroyer classes. It was not until the hard proving-ground of war that it was realised that the more urgent need was for a stronger anti-aircraft armament, and this resulted in the halving of the number of torpedoes carried. It should not be forgotten however that torpedo attacks by British destroyers were a major factor in the war at sea and often the mere threat of such an attack was sufficient to turn away superior enemy forces.

Off the Norwegian coast in June 1940 for example the two German battle-cruisers *Scharnhorst* and *Gneisenau* were both surprised by the daring manner in which *Ardent* and *Acasta* attacked with torpedoes through smoke in the face of overwhelming fire. It must be remembered that even the mere damage to one of the larger German warships in the Atlantic or similar waters where they would operate far from bases, could mean the loss of the ship. In the Mediterranean the Italians were equally cautious when tackling British destroyers as witness the battle of Sirte and the decisive action off Cape Bon in 1941. The Japanese navy was not caught lacking for they had developed their own 'Long Lance' torpedo for their destroyers, a weapon which far outclassed any torpedo in any other navy both in range, accuracy and hitting power. Skilful use of this torpedo resulted in some resounding victories over superior American forces during the Solomon Islands campaign in 1942/43. So the Admiralty were wise to press for increased torpedo armaments in destroyers.

On the outbreak of the war she was serving with the 1st Destroyer Flotilla in the Mediterranean under the command of Lieutenant-Commander G. B. Roope. When Italy decided to remain neutral for the time being, this crack flotilla was transferred back to home waters and operated from Harwich into the North Sea. Here, in the front line of the sea war, they soon suffered heavy casualties, the flotilla leader *Grenville* and *Gypsy* both being lost in the early months of 1940. The remainder of the flotilla moved to Scapa Flow in April of that year.

The Germans had long been violating the neutrality of Norwegian territoral waters by shipping cargoes of vital iron-ore along the sheltered 'Leads' to feed her war industry and the 'Altmark Incident', during which the German prison ship had been boarded and British prisoners released after months of captivity, had brought matters to a head. On the British side Winston Churchill was First Lord of the Admiralty and he resolved to stop this traffic once and for all by laying minefields off the Norwegian coast which would force German freighters out to sea and into the arms of the waiting Royal Navy. However Hitler was equally determined to thwart any British dominance of the Scandinavian area and put in hand the invasion and occupation of Norway. By coincidence, both sides initiated direct action at the same time and a confused clash resulted in the first days of April 1940.

The British minelaying sortie was codenamed Operation 'Wilfred' and on the 5th April the minelayer *Teviot Bank* sailed from Scapa Flow escorted by the battle-cruiser *Renown* and the destroyers *Greyhound*, *Glowworm*, *Hyperion* and *Hero*. They were later joined by the 20th Destroyer Flotilla of four destroyers equipped as minelayers, escorted by the 2nd Flotilla of destroyers. The whole force steamed north in vile weather with the object of laying their minefield off the Lofoten Islands in Vestfiord with the purpose of sealing the entrance to the vital port of Narvik to German shipping.

Unknown to them, the German invasion had already been put in train and also at sea, and heading for Narvik, was a strong German force consisting of *Scharnhorst*, *Gneisenau*, *Admiral Hipper* and several large destroyers. Their objective was to land troops at Narvik to occupy and hold that town while further German forces landed elsewhere along the Norwegian coast and linked up.

As the British force rolled and plunged northward on the 8th a man was swept overboard from *Glowworm*. *Renown* gave permission for a search to be made and *Glowworm* hauled round and was soon lost to sight in the heaving ocean. This was the last that British eyes were to see of the little *Glowworm*. Despite a persistent hunt, the lost crewman was never found and Lieutenant-Commander Roope resumed course to catch up with his squadron again. He never did.

On the 8th of April *Glowworm* had fallen in with a large German destroyer at dawn. Identification of the blurred shape was difficult but she was seen to be an enemy vessel and *Glowworm* fired two salvoes from her main armament before her adversary slipped back into the murk. Lieutenant-Commander Roope was completely surprised by the presence of German surface forces in this area but turned to follow and almost immediately was confronted by a second enemy destroyer, *Bernd von Arnim*. Both ships were pitching and rolling heavily in the tumbling seas but this proved to *Glowworm's* advantage, for *von Arnim* carried a heavier gun armament which made her less seaworthy and rather than stand and make a fight of it, encumbered as she was with her cargo of troops for Narvik, she also turned away, calling for assistance as she did so.

The *Glowworm* pressed on after her. If German forces were at sea in strength it was Roope's duty to find exactly in what strength and report it to the Admiralty and to the *Renown* to the north of him. For *von Arnim* help was soon on hand for out of that April morning's gloom there appeared the massive bulk of the heavy cruiser *Admiral Hipper*. 14,000 tons, ten times *Glowworm's* size and mounting eight 8-inch guns, she soon opened a devastating fire on her puny adversary. Frantic attempts were made by *Glowworm* to get off the vital signals about the German force but *Hipper's* big guns were soon scoring devastating hits on the frail British destroyer, knocking out her guns and reducing her upperworks to wreckage. Knowing that escape was impossible Roope decided to go into the attack and attempt to inflict as much damage on her mighty opponent as he could before he went down. Although heavily outgunned by the German ship, *Glowworm* still had a powerful punch with ten torpedoes if only she could survive long enough to fire them.

Making a smokescreen, *Glowworm* closed *Hipper* although frequently hit by the heavy shells. She managed to fire off a salvo of torpedoes but these *Hipper* was able to avoid by sharp alterations in course. *Glowworm* was clearly doomed but took temporary refuge behind her smokescreen. *Hipper* plunged forward to finish her off only to be met by the amazing sight of the British vessel, little more than a floating wreck, steering straight at her intent on ramming. So close was *Glowworm* that although *Hipper* again swung round hard she could not avoid being struck hard. The collision tore away 130 feet of *Hipper's* armoured belt. *Glowworm* cannoned off and lay disabled for a short while before she blew up and slipped beneath the waves. The German ships made attempts to rescue her crew in the oil drenched sea but only 38 were recovered and the gallant Roope was not among the survivors.

For this outstanding example of bravery and devotion to duty Roope was awarded the posthumous Victoria Cross, the first awarded to the Royal Navy in the Second World War and the name *Glowworm* was firmly established in the annals of the Royal Navy.

The badge features a lantern, black, with rays issuing, silver, and the motto *Ex tenebris Lux* (Out of darkness, light).

H.M.S. Hood

This is an example of a name that is equally famous in the Royal Navy for the ships and for the many famous seamen of the name that have been prominent in the service. The Hood's were one of the most prominent naval families and among the distinguished officers are included Admiral Viscount Hood, (1724-1816), Admiral Viscount Bridport, (1727-1814), Vice-Admiral Sir Samuel Hood, (1762-1814), Captain Alexander Hood (1758-1798), Admiral Lord Hood of Avalon (1824-1901) and Rear-Admiral Sir Horace Hood. The latter was the gallant officer who took his battle-cruiser *Invincible* into action at Jutland and lost his life in the split-second annihilation of that ship when she blew up and sank with all her crew save three. There is considerable irony in the fact that the mightiest ship to bear the name of Hood was also a battle-cruiser and she too was destroyed in an instant with almost her entire ship's company.

The name was therefore already an honoured one when the first ship to be so called was launched in 1859. She had an uneventful life and in 1891 the second ship took to the water. She was one of the 'Admiral' class battleships which marked the first stabilisation of battleship design for fifty years and 'wooden walls and broadsides' and sail power gave way to huge guns mounted in barbettes, thick armour and the clanking, juddering steam power of a new age. The second *Hood* survived long enough to be utilised as a blockship at the beginning of World War I.

The third and last *Hood* was the mighty battle-cruiser which was laid down in 1915 as a class of four. The concept of the battle-cruiser was that she would be fast enough to catch and destroy any enemy vessel save for the battleship, and thus she sacrificed the battleship's armour for the extra seven or eight knots, and carried the same main armament.

In practice however the battle-cruiser was used as the fast wing of the battle-fleet and thus came into direct contact with the more powerfully protected battleships. In a straight duel the consequences were tragic and no less than three British battle-cruisers were lost at Jutland due to insufficient armour.

Hood was designed before Jutland was fought, but as she was not finally completed until 1920 it was thought that she embodied the lessons thus learnt. Certainly she was the most powerful warship of her day and her displacement of 41,200 tons made far and away the heaviest capital ship in the world for twenty years. Additional protection was worked into her design, but what was considered ample to protect her in 1920 was hardly adequate twenty years later. At the range of seven-and-a-half miles at which *Invincible* met her end the shells were striking her deck armour at a plunging angle rather than horizontally. In 1941 *Bismarck* opened fire on *Hood* at 25,000 yards, almost twice the range, which meant that her 15-inch one-ton armour piercing shells were striking the target almost vertically.

In 1920, when she joined the fleet, *Hood* had a reputation for invincibility due to her size. She was also a beautiful ship, perfectly proportioned, with a striking flare to the bows. The Washington Navy Treaty of 1922 limited the size of new battleships to 35,000 tons displacement so there was no question of any larger vessel disputing her position as 'Queen of the Seas'. Her first voyage was a visit to Scandinavia in 1920 and in 1922, under the command of Rear-Admiral Cowan, she cruised to South American and West Indian ports with the *Repulse*.

In 1923 these same two vessels, accompanied by the 1st Light Cruiser Squadron, undertook a round-the-world cruise which was most successful and helped re-establish links with the Commonwealth after the Great War. She then served with the Home Fleet until 1935. Following a short refit she joined the Mediterranean Fleet, spending much of her time up to 1939 off the coast of Spain protecting British merchant shipping during the Spanish Civil War. After another short refit she joined the Home Fleet at Scapa Flow where she was when war was declared. During all this long period plans were made to modernise her, increase her deck armour protection and give her a more sophisticated secondary armament but the money was never available and she was therefore little better equipped in 1939 than in 1920.

Some idea of the amount of reconstruction considered in 1939 for *Hood*, in order to bring her back into the front line can be gauged by noting that she was to be equipped with new machinery and her underwater protection was to be modified. The torpedo tubes, which battleships had carried for so long as useless encumbrances, were to be removed, as was her armoured conning tower. Both her 5.5-inch and her 4-inch guns were to be taken out and replaced with the modern dual purpose 5.25-inch guns. Hangars were to be fitted to carry seaplanes. This however would have proved a wasted modification, for most warships fitted to carry these aircraft subsequently abandoned them during the war when aircraft carriers provided both scouting and fighter aircraft for the fleet. With the reduction in tonnage brought about by the removal of some of her needless top-weight it was planned to increase both her vertical and horizontal armoured protection which might have been decisive.

However it was not to be, for the idea of laying-up the Royal Navy's largest warship for over two years while these modifications were made to her was not considered feasible in the late 1930's. With the war plainly imminent Britain could not afford to have a vessel like *Hood* out of service for such a long period until the new battleships under construction joined the fleet and this was not due until 1940 and 1941. So she stayed as she was.

In times of peace the voting of money for defence is always a tardy proposition for any Government and in the 'tween war period the development of the strength of the Navy was restricted by numerous complications. Firstly there was the adverse economic climate, with the depression of the early 1930's only slowly being overcome. Then there were the numerous naval conferences which took place in this period, all of which appeared to result in further limitations on the size of the fleet. The major factor in replacing old tonnage with new was Winston Churchill's 'Ten Year' ruling, made with the optimistic forecast of no major war for ten years. It was recurring and so the ten years envisaged peace rolled on into eternity and money was therefore withheld. When it was belatedly realised that war, far from being ten years into the future in 1937, was imminent, the bulk of the new funds made available were urgently needed in a massive programme of new construction to make up the fifteen years of standstill and little could be spared for *Hood*.

Her very size and legend of power tended to mark her as a special unit and the press, having for so many years championed her as the most powerful ship in the world hardly wished to point out her deficiencies so late in the day.

So *Hood* had to be content with a refit which lasted from February to August 1939 and she was able to commission again just before the start of World War II as the Flagship of Vice Admiral Sir W. J. Whitworth.

During an early patrol with the Home Fleet in the North Sea in 1939 *Hood* was struck by a 500-lb bomb which glanced off without causing any damage and in the first months of 1940 she was refitting at Plymouth. On completion of this, after the fall of France, she sailed for Gibraltar where she became the flagship of Admiral Sir James Somerville for a short period. Under him she took part in the tragic destruction of the French Fleet under Vichy control at Mers-el-Kebir near Oran in July. After this she carried out a sortie into the Mediterranean before heavy air attacks made her turn back to Gibraltar.

In September *Hood* returned to Scapa Flow and spent the winter of 1940-41 on patrols in the northern waters around Iceland watching over any attempted break out by German heavy units. She was thus still employed in May 1941 when *Bismarck* and *Prinz Eugen* got through our patrols. *Hood* and the brand-new battleship *Prince of Wales* were despatched to intercept and destroy the German ships before they broke loose on the British convoy routes.

The two British ships sighted the German squadron early on the 24th and at once steered to engage. Aboard the shadowing cruisers the sight of *Hood* appearing out of the haze seemed to indicate that the end was in sight for the German squadron but such was not the case. Fire was opened at 5.52 at a range of 25,000 yards and *Hood* and *Prince of Wales* were steering towards *Bismarck* to close the range. They could not therefore utilise the whole of the main armament for the guns astern of the ships were masked by the superstructure.

The German ship at once replied very accurately and on her third salvo she hit *Hood* close to her mainmast setting her on fire. At 5.55 the British ships began to turn broadside on to the Germans to enable all guns to open fire. As they did so *Bismarck's* fifth salvo struck *Hood* with devastating effect. A thousand feet high explosion tore her asunder and she split in two sinking in less than two minutes. There were only three survivors from her crew of 1,415 officers and men.

H.M.S. Marlborough

The famous soldier and ancestor of Sir Winston Churchill, John Churchill, Duke of Marlborough and the victor of the battles of Blenheim, Malplaquet, Oudenarde and Ramillies, is the man from whom this famous name derives. The first vessel to so honour him in the Royal Navy was the 2nd-rate *St. Michael* which was renamed *Marlborough* in 1702. She fought at the battles of Toulon in 1744 and was with the fleet in the West Indies during the battles at Martinique and the capture of Havana in 1762 when she flew the flag of Rear-Admiral Rodney. Unfortunately she was abandoned and destroyed at sea the same year.

One of the ubiquitous 3rd-rates was the next to carry the name. She was launched in 1767 and was present at many of the great sea fights of the late 18th-century, including in her many battle honours those of St. Vincent in 1780, The Saintes in 1782 and the Glorious First of June in 1794. Like her predecessor however she met an unhappy end being wrecked in 1800.

She was followed into service by another 3rd-rate *Marlborough* of 1807. She served for almost thirty years and was broken up in 1835. Such a distinguished name was not long unallocated however for a large 1st rate battleship took the water in 1855. She was one of the very last of our "Line of Battle" ships for within a few years of her completion she was already completely obsolete, her mighty oaken hull and tiers of cannon having been surpassed by the iron built hulls of *Black Prince* and *Warrior*. Despite this she lingered on in the service in secondary roles for half a century before being hulked as part of the *Vernon* establishment in 1904. She was finally sold out in 1924 but on the way to the breakers the ancient vessel capsized and broke in half.

The next ship to carry the proud name *Marlborough* was entirely different from the fourth but was still built as a battleship, albeit of a very different era. She was one of the great 'Iron Duke' class vessels, a sister ship to *Benbow* described earlier, displacing 25,000 tons and carrying ten 13.5 inch guns at 21 knots. Their main feature was that they were the last British battleships to be built exclusively as coal burning vessels. It is perhaps not realised what a handicap this was. After days patrolling in the North Sea the battle squadrons would return to harbour after being buffeted by severe weather only to have their exhausted crews turn to the coal ship ready for the next sortie. This was a filthy and protracted operation in which everyone took part dressed in their oldest clothes. The collier would come alongside and the coal had to be transhipped in small sacks and manhandled down the chutes. By contrast subsequent ships which were oil-fired simply coupled up their hoses. The main reason that coal was retained for so long was that supplies were secure whereas oil had to be transported long distances from the Middle East and tankers were few. The most powerful factor for the continued use of coal was put forward as being the amount of protection the full bunkers could provide for a ship. The main armour belts of *Marlborough* were 12-inches thick along the waterline, thinning to 8-inches below and from 9 to 6-inches above. The coal bunkers backing this armour were up to seventeen feet wide and gave protection to the vulnerable boiler room spaces whereas the engine rooms and magazines relied on 1½-inch thick armour side screens.

The effectiveness of full coal bunkers as a method of stopping a torpedo is fully demonstrated by *Marlborough* herself. She was struck amidships by a torpedo at the battle of Jutland. A hole some seventy feet wide by twenty feet deep was torn in her hull but despite this she was able to continue in action at seventeen knots.

Although all subsequent battleships were built to burn oil fuel it is interesting to note that when the *Royal Sovereign* class were designed some years after *Marlborough* and her sisters, they were to be coal burning battleships due to the uncertainty of oil supplies during wartime conditions. However with the return of Fisher to the Admiralty such a backward step was immediately modified.

This fifth *Marlborough* was the vessel whose badge and crest is here depicted and she was built at Devonport Dockyard between January 1912 and June 1914, joining the Grand Fleet just at the outbreak of the First World War. She was with the 1st Battle Squadron, being the flagship of Admiral Sir Lewis Bayly until December 1914 when he was replaced by Vice-Admiral Sir Cecil Burney. She was present at the Battle of Jutland and was one of the first of the Grand Fleet battleships to open fire. She was also the only British battleship to receive damage from a torpedo during that battle.

At 6.57 she was hit by a torpedo from the disabled German light cruiser *Wiesbaden* which struck her under the forebridge in her diesel engine room and reducing her speed to 17 knots. She was still able to use her main armament however and stayed in line with a list of seven degrees to starboard. She survived three more torpedo attacks during the main action and was attacked twice more by submarine torpedoes the next day while on her way to Immingham to repair the damage but came through without further mishap.

Like *Benbow* she served with the Mediterranean Fleet post-war following a major refit in 1920-21. After service with the Atlantic Fleet until 1929 she was reduced to reserve and sold out for scrap in May 1932. Again, as with her sister, the name was not revived for a ship but for a shore establishment, that of the Torpedo School at Eastbourne College 1942-47.

H.M.S. Nelson

The name of the third of our trio of famous battleships was an obviously popular one in the service after the death of the great hero of the Nile, Copenhagen and Trafalgar. The lion rampant regardant, holding in his paw a palm branch, is adapted from one of the supporters of the arms of Lord Nelson. The motto is *Palmam Qui Meruit Ferat* (Let him bear the palm who has deserved it).

The name itself dates from 1799 and has been alternately given to many great ships as *Lord Nelson* and *Nelson*. Three small vessels bore the name *Lord Nelson* but the first major vessel was the 1st rate battleship *Nelson* launched in 1814. She served for a great number of years before finally being presented to the Government of the State of Victoria in Australia in 1867.

A cruiser was the next ship to be called *Nelson* and she was one of the interesting hybrid types which so proliferated in the late 19th-century. She was the last British capital ship to carry her main armament on the broadside and between decks in the old traditional manner and was the first to be built with the 'protective' deck at each end. She carried a three masted rig in addition to variable compound engines which gave her a speed of 14 knots.

She was built by Elder and Company, being laid down in November 1874 and completed in July 1881 at a cost of £411,302. She shipped four 10-inch 18-ton guns, and eight 9-inch 12 ton guns and had an armour belt of 9-inch maximum thickness with a 2-inch deck. She had a crew of 560 and displaced 7,500 tons. Like many of their contemporaries, *Nelson*, and her sister ship, *Northampton*, were ships of undetermined functions or abilities and of little practical value to the fleet save for experimentation.

They were described alternately as 'armoured ships', 'protected cruisers' and, more succinctly by the captain of one of them, as a 'sham'. Nevertheless these unhappy attempts at combining the role of commerce protecting cruiser and 3rd-rate battleship kept them employed on the more distant stations for a number of years before being relegated to subsidiary duties. *Nelson* herself served on the Australian station as Commodore's ship between 1882 and 1885, was fitted out as flagship and did not return home until 1889. She was given a 'modernisation' at Chatham during the next three years which gave her the outward appearance of a fighting vessel, which she was not, even when fitted with four 4.7-inch quick-firing guns. She served subsequently as guardship at Portsmouth and then as flagship at Sheerness, taking part, in all seriousness, in the annual manoeuvres until 1893 when she went into reserve. She performed trooping runs to Malta before being hulked as a stokers' training ship. She was finally sold out in 1910.

The next major fighting unit to carry the name was *Lord Nelson*, a battleship completed in October 1908. She was also an unfortunate ship for, like her predecessor, she was useless before she was completed. She had the misfortune to be the last of the old 'pre-Dreadnought' types of battleship with a basic design resting on four 12-inch guns and 18 knots speed. Judged by these standards she was an excellent warship for she introduced the big 9.2-inch gun to battleship design as an alternative to her main armament. While it is true that earlier battleships had mounted this weapon *Lord Nelson* carried no less than ten of these guns in large turrets to supplement her four 12-inch guns and she looked a powerful vessel bristling with weapons. She was the last battleship to have the old reciprocating engines but her real misfortune, and that of her sister ship *Agamemnon* was that she was not completed until *after* the all big gun *Dreadnought* had been in commission for some time, and the reaction to the expenditure of some £1,540,000 on a battleship already completely outclassed raised no little comment among the general public.

They both nonetheless saw considerable service, *Lord Nelson* serving with the Home Fleet up to 1914 and on the outbreak of war was flagship of the Channel Fleet protecting the transportation of the B.E.F. to France. The next year she went out to the Dardanelles, again as flagship, and remained in the Mediterranean for the rest of the war. She returned to Sheerness in May 1919 and was sold out the following year.

Nelson which followed in 1927 showed a big advance over the earlier ship. Although cut down in size and speed from the original design, the new *Nelson* was to remain the largest and most heavily armed battleship in the fleet for over twelve years. The Washington Treaty of 1922 resulted in the wholesale scrapping of the bulk of the almost impregnable Royal Navy which existed in 1919. In all, Britain scrapped 657 ships displacing one-and-a-half million tons. The poor skeleton of the fleet as it remained was equal in size to the navy of the United States, a relative newcomer to naval affairs on the front line, and only marginally larger than that of Japan. Never again would the Royal Navy stand supreme as *the* naval power. The ships built to replace the older vessels were all subject to strict treaty limitations, but unfortunately Britain was the only nation to take them seriously.

Nelson and her sister ship *Rodney* displaced 33,950 tons and carried the new 16-inch gun, nine being mounted in three triple turrets. Her speed was only 21 knots as the reduced size of the ship meant that if modern guns and armour were to be carried speed must be sacrificed.

The main armament was concentrated forward in three triple turrets and this arrangement enabled the magazine armour to be concentrated. The loss of an astern arc was accepted and although in theory the after turrets could train abeam the blast effect from the 16-inch guns in this position made the bridge untenable and thus the use of the guns was further restricted. These guns had an elevation of forty degrees and so were, in theory, adaptable for use against aircraft, and during the war full broadsides of 16-inch shells were fired at aircraft targets, both in daylight, to lay down a shell splash barrier to deter low-flying torpedo bombers, and at night in a blind barrage, the effects of which were shattering. They had an extreme range of 35,000 yards, and the cost of each full salvo was £700.

Her armoured belt was of 14-inch thickness and angled while her deck armour was of 6¼-inch thickness, more than sufficient to keep out the puny bombs envisaged in the 1920's but quite inadequate of course ten years later. Considerable attempts were made to offset the strict treaty limitations on tonnage and so much were they cut back that they were eventually over a 1,000 tons lighter than permitted.

They were powered by Brown-Curtis geared turbines with a designed h.p. of 45,000, despite which they were only good for 21 knots in service. They had eight 3-drum type boilers and had an oil bunkerage of 4,000 tons. Both *Nelson* and *Rodney* were fitted out as flagships and *Nelson* spent a large part of her active life in this role. Their complements were given officially as 1,361 which in wartime would be increased to 1,640 officers and men. Her total cost was £7,504,055.

With her single funnel and huge mass of bridge, christened in the fleet 'Queen Anne's Mansions' after a well known London block, she presented a unique profile among British warships, and until the advent of the *Tiger* helicopter cruiser, conversions of the late 60's, was considered among the ugliest of warship designs. They were also unique internally when built as being the first battleships built for the Royal Navy with the engines located forward of the boiler rooms.

Nelson was built by Armstrongs and completed in June 1927 and no other battleships were built for the next thirteen years. She commissioned on 15th August 1927 and for the next fourteen years wore the flag of seven successive Commanders-in-Chief, serving with the Atlantic and Home Fleets.

She was thus serving at the outbreak of World War Two and in December of 1939 she was one of the first, and most serious, casualties of the new magnetic mine. She did not rejoin the fleet until August 1940. She continued to serve with the Home Fleet although in 1941 and 1942 she was detached as flagship of Force 'H' to fight through the large Malta Convoys 'Halberd' and 'Pedestal' and received damage from an aerial torpedo during the former.

She supported the landings in North Africa in late 1942 and carried out bombardment duties in support of the landings in Sicily and at Salerno. The Italian surrender was signed aboard the *Nelson* by Eisenhower in September 1943 while at anchor at Malta. In June 1944 she was present at the Normandy landings giving invaluable fire support. She was damaged by a mine and was repaired in the United States. After this she sailed for the East Indies to become the flagship of the East Indies Fleet and the surrender of the Japanese forces in Malaya was signed at the same table aboard her as was the Italian surrender.

On return to England after the war *Nelson* served for two years as training battleship before being sold and used as a bombing target before going to the breakers yard in the autumn of 1948 after a period of service of over twenty years.

It is of interest to note that the battle honours awarded to *Nelson*, as indeed to any warship which bears the name of a famous sailor, are only those accredited to the ship itself. Therefore *Nelson* is not entitled to wear the battle honours of any of Admiral Nelson's actions, which go to the ships which were actually present at the time, *Victory*, etc. This is a point that is often overlooked, when naming warships.

H.M.S. Renown

This very famous ship carries the motto *Antiquae Famae Custos* which means 'Guardian of Ancient Renown' and is an historic name in the Royal navy. It originated as a prize name when the twenty gun French *Renommée* was captured in 1651. France refused to recognise the Commonwealth of Oliver Cromwell and when the French began molesting English shipping Cromwell ordered his Generals-at-Sea to carry out reprisals. The *Renommée* was taken and served under her new name in the Royal Navy throughout the wars with the Dutch which followed, serving at the battles of Gabbard and Scheveningen in 1653, before being discarded the following year.

A century later, with remarkable coincidence, another French *Renommée* was taken as a prize in 1747, serving with the fleet for over twenty years before being broken up in 1771. The name was now honourably established in the Royal Navy and in 1774 a 4th-rate was launched as *Renown* and she saw action at Ushant on December 12th 1781. Again she served for twenty years before going to the breakers.

In 1793 the new Republic of France declared war on Britain and Holland and their armies soon began to overrun Europe. At sea the Royal Navy commenced its usual patient blockade and the following year a fleet under Admiral Sir John Jervis was sent to the West Indies to take the French islands there. It was during this period of sea fighting that the third French *Renommée* to be captured by the British was taken, in 1796, and again added to the Royal Navy under her own name. She was a 5th-rate and served for fourteen years under her new flag, being present during the Egyptian campaign of 1801. She was broken up in 1810.

It was during this critical period in the nation's history that two vessels bearing this name, albeit one spelt in French, were at sea with the fleet, for in 1798 a new 3rd-rate took to the water named *Renown*. The 3rd rate had become increasingly popular in the fleet, being a two-decker carrying eighty guns. She was thus not too weak to stand in the line-of-battle if needed but also was handy enough to operate independently and was much cheaper to build. Thus the great expansion of the fleet forced by the Napoleonic wars was greatly facilitated by adding many of these types to back up the larger 100-gun 1st-rates. *Renown* gave good service before being broken up in 1835.

The Royal Navy had, by a series of overwhelming victories against the French and Spanish, become pre-eminent among the world's fleets and this position was to remain unchallenged for over one hundred years. Thus it was that when the sixth vessel to bear the name, a large 2nd rate battleship, was launched in 1857, she began a largely uneventful lifespan and saw no major action in her long life. She went to the breakers in 1870.

If there was little action in which to test the mettle of the Navy in the Victorian era then there was much to disturb it from a technical point of view for with the development of steam power, the adoption of armour and the great strides forward made in gunnery and the new invention of the torpedo, the very future of the line-of-battle ship seemed in grave doubt. From a welter of half-formed ideas and experiments the design of British battleships was stabilised for a time with the appearance of the *Royal Sovereign* class in 1892. Under the direction of Sir William White the navy began a steady building programme which gave them the two for one strength on which the safety of the Empire for a long period rested. This meant in effect that the strength of the Royal Navy was at all times to be maintained at a level equal or superior to the next two strongest naval powers. At this period the rivals were France and Russia, although Germany, Japan and the United States were to become increasingly obvious candidates over the following decades.

The Royal Navy, built to defend an empire which was world wide, had to be prepared for combat anywhere and it was with this possibility in mind that Sir William White designed the next *Renown*. She was a much smaller version of the current battleship design and was built specifically to operate on the more distant stations, her shallow draught being designed so that she could pass through the Suez Canal. She was launched at Pembroke Dockyard in 1895 and completed ready for sea in January 1897. On a 10,500 ton displacement she mounted four 10 inch guns in two hooded barbettes, with a secondary armament of ten 6-inch guns in casements. She cost a total of £709,000 which was much cheaper than contemporary full-scale battleships.

She was always a popular ship in the fleet and had a reputation for smartness which always outshone her larger sisters. She was the flagship of Sir John Fisher on the North American and West Indies station and later in the Mediterranean. In 1902 she had a special refit and took the Duke and Duchess of Connaught to India as representatives of the King at the Delhi Durbar. She performed the same function in 1905 when her guests for the voyage to India were the then Prince and Princess of Wales, later King George V and Queen Mary. After such a distinguished early life she finished her days somewhat forlornly as a stokers training ship and was scrapped in 1913.

The name was kept alive after this but it was the ninth *Renown* which was to become the most famous of them all. This was the battle-cruiser built under the direction of Admiral 'Jackie' Fisher and completed just after the battle of Jutland in 1916. This battle had shown the terrible weakness of the battle-cruiser type, which had been built for speed, when exposed to concentrated fire from battleships and because of this *Renown* and her sister *Repulse* were looked on as white elephants when they joined the Grand Fleet. They were not however put to the ultimate test in the First World War and, because of their speed of 32 knots, were retained post-war. In the late 1930's with the threat of war with Germany again looming *Renown* was extensively rebuilt and emerged as a first-class fighting unit.

This refit took place between 1936 and 1939 at a cost of £3,088,008 and entailed the preparation of the old ship to face the threat of air attack, thicker armour to protect her vulnerable magazines and machinery and better protection against torpedo attack. The elevation of the main armament was increased to give her better range and her old secondary armament was replaced by a superb system of twenty 4.5 inch guns in twin turrets and three eight barrelled pom-poms for close-range defence.

Of course even this armament, although quite excellent for 1939, had to have numerous additions made to it in the light of wartime knowledge and she eventually carried another sixty-four 20mm oerlikon guns and another mulitiple pom-pom. The extra weight this heavy armament entailed was compensated for by the replacement of her old machinery with modern equipment including small-tube high-pressure boilers. Although, even so, she came out slower than originally built, *Renown* was still the fastest capital ship in the Royal Navy and remained so throughout the war. She could not however catch the German battle-cruisers nor the new Italian battleships and all showed her a clean pair of heels.

Like *Hood*, *Renown's* sister ship *Repulse*, was not to receive a similar modification due to the outbreak of the war, and in passing it is interesting to notice that almost all the Navy's capital ship losses were those which had not been fully modernised before the war, *Hood*, *Repulse*, *Royal Oak* and *Barham*, the one exception being the *Prince of Wales* which was sent to face the world's finest torpedo-bomber force without air cover or adequate anti-aircraft armament.

The *Renown*, like *Warspite*, was certainly to justify the money spent and saw an enormous amount of front-line action during the war years.

She joined the Home Fleet and in 1940 she was in action off Norway against the brand-new German battle-cruisers *Scharnhorst* and *Gneisenau*. In a blinding snowstorm the twenty-four year old vessel chased both these ships in a confused duel before losing contact. Morale was thus high and her reputation firmly established when she joined the flag of Admiral Sir James Somerville in the famous Force 'H' based on Gibraltar.

For the next year she was constantly in action covering convoys to Malta and sweeps in the Atlantic. At the battle of Spartivento in November 1940 she repeated her performance of April when she pursued the brand-new Italian battleship *Vittoria Veneto* to within thirty miles of the Italian coast. The following year she escorted the *Ark Royal* during the *Bismark* hunt. After much service in the European theatre of operations she went out to join the East Indies Fleet in 1944 and there had a go at the third Axis partner by bombarding the Japanese held port of Sabang in the Dutch East Indies. She was finally struck off the Navy List in 1948 after 32 years of arduous service.

The present *Renown* is one of the four most powerful warships ever to serve with the Royal Navy for she is a nuclear powered submarine armed with the frightening Polaris ballistic missile. She has sixteen of these, each with a nuclear warhead ranged on a pre-determined target in Soviet Russia. As such she and her three sisters represent Britain's deterrent against aggression. It is an ironical fact that if the present *Renown* ever sees combat then her whole function will have been in vain, and there will be no battle honours after such an action.

C

H.M.S. Rocket

This badge carries with it the motto *Upward and Onward* and the design relates to Stephenson's famous steam engine. It has always been a small ship name and dates from 1804. In that year the name was given to a small 62 ton merchant ship purchased for use as a fire ship. Although fitted out for this duty she was never used and was sold three years later.

In 1842 the second *Rocket* was built at Limehouse. She was of 70 tons displacement and steam powered. She joined the fleet at Portsmouth as a general auxiliary craft and towing craft. She served in these capacities there and at Sheerness in 1848 before being scrapped at Woolwich in 1850.

The name was then given to two Crimea gunboats. The first was a 156 ton ship built at Blackwall in 1855. Designated a Mortar Vessel, she was sent instead to the Baltic during the war against Russia and took part in the bombardment of Sveaborg. The second was a steam gunboat built especially for the Crimea War. She was built at Portsmouth in 1856 and was of 235 tons. On commissioning the third *Rocket* was respecified in the fleet as Mortar Vessel 22 and she was broken up in 1865. Meanwhile the fourth *Rocket* had preceded her to the scrapyard for she was completed too late for service and, no other use being found for her, went into reserve before being scrapped in 1864. Although this may seem a wasteful process it was inevitable that a large number of specialist small craft are always required for every war, witness the landing craft of World War II, and always after a major conflict no useful duties are found for such craft.

Another gunboat followed. She was of 465 tons and was built on the Thames in 1868 and went into reserve at Woolwich on completion. After three years she was commissioned and joined the squadron based on the Cape of Good Hope. After service off the African coast she was transferred to the Pacific Station spending a part of her service working along the western seaboard of North America during which time she mounted a punitive expedition against an Indian tribe in British Columbia. *Rocket* finally returned to Home Waters in 1883, was paid off at Sheerness in June of that year and sold five years later without seeing additional service.

In 1894 the name passed to a destroyer and it is with destroyers that the name has since remained and become famous. Following the successful trials of the first two destroyers, *Havock* and *Hornet* in 1893, a large building programme was initiated to construct ships of similar design to offset the menace of the large numbers of foreign torpedo boats. *Rocket, Shark* and *Surly* were a part of this order and of a group of the earliest destroyers which later became known generally as the '27-knotters'. This was the speed they were designed for but none of them ever in fact achieved it except perhaps on trials without armament and with hand picked coal and stokers. These three were built by the firm of J & G Thomson on the Clyde and the others of the same group came from no less than thirteen other builders. It was the Admiralty policy to spread the contracts over as wide a range of constructors as possible in order to have the maximum number available with the expertise for later expansion programmes. Unfortunately the building of such specialist high speed craft was not easy and many firms went to the wall trying to meet the specifications on speed.

Rocket was 200 feet long and had a beam of 19½ feet with a displacement of 280 tons and cost about £34,000 when she was completed in 1895. She was armed with one 12-pdr and five 6-pdr guns and two single 18-inch torpedo tubes. She was powered by triple expansion engines and carried sixty tons of coal. She joined the fleet as a sea-going tender to the Detached Squadron for evaluation trials in 1896 and was present at the Naval Review a year later. She then went out to Bermuda for a spell before returning home to serve as tender to *Crescent* and in 1903 she was attached to the Vernon Torpedo School. She remained in the Portsmouth flotilla until 1912 when she was considered worn out and was sold for scrap.

The seventh *Rocket* was also a destroyer and was built by Denny Brothers of Dumbarton under the sixth order of Admiralty Design vessels built under the War Emergency Programme. She belonged to the Admiralty 'R' class and was launched in July 1916. The destroyers of this class displaced some 1,070 tons and carried an armament of three 4-inch guns and a pom-pom with 21-inch torpedo tubes. They were powered by geared turbines developing 27,000 S.H.P. which gave them a designed speed of 36 knots. The bulk of the 'R' class went first to the Grand Fleet and then to Harwich where they ended the war and *Rocket* herself was employed on the normal escort duties and on convoys to Holland. At the Armistice she was one of the British destroyers that helped escort German destroyers to surrender and was later laid up in reserve at Portsmouth before being sold for scrap after only ten years service in 1927.

The eighth and last *Rocket* was also an Emergency War Programme destroyer on this occasion the much smaller programme of 1942 when she was one of the eight ships of the 4th Emergency Flotilla, the *Rotherham* class. She was built by Scotts shipyard and launched in October 1942. With a displacement of 1,705 tons she carried four single 4.7-inch, a pom-pom and six oerlikon guns and eight 21-inch torpedo tubes. She had a complement of 175 men, twice that of her predecessor, and was powered by two-shaft geared turbines developing some 40,000 S.H.P. giving her a speed of 36¾ knots.

One novel feature of this class of destroyer was that the officers were no longer berthed aft. It was intended that the new arrangement should stay as it thus enabled the officers to reach the bridge more quickly in an emergency. It had been tried in the 'Hunt' class ships and favourable reports had been received but in practice it 'felt' wrong and very few officers liked the new arrangement. The construction of these vessels was somewhat delayed for at the time of their building a large number of older destroyers had received severe damage off Dunkirk and Norway and the 'R' class was held up on the slips while these were repaired and got quickly back to sea. So it was that contracts were not placed until December 1940. In order to speed delivery these vessels were armed with old 4.7-inch guns of which considerable numbers were on hand. It was unfortunate that although these old guns were good surface weapons they were not anti-aircraft guns.

The secondary armament was somewhat improved and consisted of a quadruple 2-pdr pom-pom sited abaft the funnel which gave a good arc of fire to dive-bombers coming in over the stern, and six single oerlikons. With this improved defence against aircraft the fact that the main armament reverted to the low-angle gun was not quite as important as it would have otherwise appeared in a ship going to war in 1943. By this date also an increasing number of carriers were joining the fleet so that fighter cover was not as sparse or unrelated as had been the case with R.A.F. aircraft operating at long distances from land bases.

All the same with the advent of the Kamikaze it was realised that the 20mm oerlikon was not a heavy enough weapon to stop a determined pilot and later in the war *Rocket* and her sisters adopted the bofors 40mm gun as it became available. Also, as complete, they had graceful tripod masts, but the ever increasing amount of radar and associated gear shipped resulted in most of them having this replaced with a heavy lattice mast which somewhat marred their appearance.

Her first action took place in the English Channel and was not a successful one at all. A force consisting of the light cruiser *Charybdis* and six destroyers was sent to hunt the German blockade runner *Munsterland* between Brest and Cherbourg on the night of the 22nd/23rd October. They were picked up by German coastal radar and intercepted by a German destroyer flotilla of five ships. Both *Charybdis* and the destroyer *Limbourne* were struck by torpedoes, the former sinking with heavy casualties while the latter had to be sunk by *Rocket* and *Talybont*. There was some confusion in the British squadron after this and no retaliation was made. Indeed the German vessels watched the rescue work and could easily have inflicted further damage had they so wished. *Munsterland* continued her voyage unmolested while the *Rocket* and her sisters returned with the survivors.

Service in the Mediterranean followed and in early 1944 she went out to join the Eastern Fleet where she took part in the destroyer attack which accompanied the bombardment and air strikes against Sabang in Japanese held Sumatra in July. She continued to work with the Eastern Fleet and was present during the air strike made by carriers of the fleet against Sigli that September and in the bombardment of Port Blair in the Andaman Islands in March 1945. At the war's end she returned home and was placed in reserve. She was one of the destroyers selected to be reduced to a frigate in the early 1950's when her armament was removed, her upperworks rebuilt and extra anti-submarine equipment was built into her. In this new role she served on into the late 1960's before reducing to reserve and being broken up after over twenty-five years service.

H.M.S. Sea Lion

The name originated in the Great War but such an obvious 'submersible' choice was naturally soon transferred to a submarine. This *Sea Lion* was one of the original 'S' class submarines built between 1932 and 1937 and was the first attempt at producing a standard design following inter-war experimentation with much larger types.

They displaced 670 tons surfaced and 960 tons submerged and had a length of 208¾ feet overall with a breadth of 24 feet. The *Sea Lion* carried a crew of 38 and was driven by two shaft Diesel/Electric motors which gave them a submerged speed of ten knots and a surfaced speed of fourteen knots. They were armed with a single 3-inch gun and six 21-inch torpedo tubes, all fixed bow mountings. *Sea Lion* herself was built by Cammell Laird and launched in March 1934.

Although small and slow by present day standards the 'S' class boats proved themselves most useful patrol craft in the restricted waters of the North Sea and the Mediterranean and so popular did they become that on the outbreak of war a massive programme was put in hand to build scores more based on this proven design.

Sea Lion herself had a most active war service as witness the battle honours of North Sea 1940, Norway 1940-41 and Arctic 1941-42 with which she is officially credited. Of the twelve original submarines of her class she was one of two only which survived the war, all the others being casualties.

Sea Lion was in the Mediterranean on the outbreak of war but quickly brought back home to begin operations against the heavily defended German North Sea sealanes early in 1940. In April of that year while en route to her patrol area in the Skagerrak she sighted and chased the German minelayer *Ulm* but failed to catch her. After her brush with the *Ulm*, *Sea Lion* had better fortune on the 11th April when she penetrated into the Kattegat and was rewarded with the sinking of the German transport *August Leonhardt*.

During the winter of 1941 *Sea Lion*, under the command of Lieutenant G. R. Colvin, was one of the submarines selected to be based at the Russian naval base at Murmansk in the Arctic Circle to help the not very efficient Russian naval forces to intercept German supply vessels. In spite of terrible weather conditions the submarines patrolled throughout the winter months on this duty with very little co-operation. Rear-Admiral Chalmers has described the conditions under which *Sea Lion* went to war: —

> "For them conditions were worse; practically no daylight, very poor visi-
> bility in the short hours of twilight, and violent storms with snow and
> sleet most of the night. Air reconnaissance being absent, the submarines
> could keep their watch on the surface, but everything was frozen solid."

Sea Lion was withdrawn in January 1942 but her next patrol was no sinecure either. For months the German battle-cruisers *Scharnhorst* and *Gneisenau* had been bottled up in harbour at Brest in France, but it had become obvious that they intended to break out again. It was known that after such a prolonged period in harbour some rudimentary training would have to be undertaken before they attempted such a sortie and the gallant *Sea Lion* was ordered to patrol right inside the very dangerous exercise area, right under the noses of the German defences and beset by the natural hazards of this part of the French coast.

This Lieutenant Colvin did on the nights of the 9th and 10th February 1942, constantly being forced to dive from German aircraft patrols. Eventually he was forced to withdraw from the area in order to replenish his depleted batteries. This he did on the 11th/12th and it was by cruel chance that this was the night selected by the Germans for the famous 'Channel Dash' when the two German giants accompanied by the cruiser *Prinz Eugen* steamed through the English Channel to Germany unharmed by R.A.F. Bomber Command and such light naval forces as were on hand.

By 1943 *Sea Lion* was no longer fit for front-line duties but she continued to play a surprisingly active role and a very useful one in the training of submarine crews for the newer boats then coming into service. Her last duty was that of a submarine target and she was thus expended in attacks during March 1945.

Her name was passed on in the late 1950's to a new type of conventional submarine which embodied many of the lessons learnt during the war. The new *Sea Lion* however is only a temporary stop-gap until sufficient nuclear-powered submarines enter service, for even though equipped with vastly superior devices to those of her predecessor she is out of date in terms of modern sea warfare.

The present *Sea Lion* however is a useful craft in limited fields, being fast and silent running. Armed only with conventional torpedoes and with a streamlined hull form she is used quite extensively in a training role as a target vessel for the new frigates. None of the post-war submarines is equipped to carry a gun, underwater speed being considered the overriding factor, but recent developments in anti-submarine helicopters have led to the development of a small missile which can be fired from a submerged submarine at periscope depth against such a menace. Called the *Blowpipe* it is small enough to be carried by submarines of the *Sea Lion* type.

The badge features a seahorse, gold and the motto *Sis ut Leones* means, 'Be like the Lions'.

H.M.S. Sesame

To make a comprehensive book on naval heraldry one must not merely include the most famous ships and the most impressive badge designs. For completeness our work also contains examples of ships badges which to the student of naval history and warship names are merely delightful rather than awe-inspiring. Two such are mentioned here, the little destroyers *Sesame* and *Stormcloud*.

Both belonged to the same class, the 'S' class of the First World War. These were good looking little vessels of around 1,000 tons displacement, and were a continuation of the basic wartime design which started in 1914 with the 'M' class which was steadily improved throughout hostilities. All carried the same basic armament of three 4-inch guns and one 2-pdr. pom-pom together with four 21 inch torpedo tubes. With a complement of ninety men, a length of 275 feet and designed for 36 knots they were simple to produce, were of an all-round efficient, economical and war-proven design and could be mass-produced by the score.

The 'S' class differed from earlier types by mounting two single 14-inch torpedo tubes at the break in the forecastle, designed to be fired ahead during fast, close-range actions in the Channel but these were later removed. Also to give better sea-going qualities their forecastles were flared forward and slightly turtle-backed and their funnels were slightly raised to alleviate smoke problems.

All who served in the 'S' class loved them. Here is what Admiral of the Fleet Viscount Cunningham of Hyndhope had to say about the *Seafire:* —

"She was a fine seaboat and fast in all weathers—33 knots 'all out' when it was not blowing. To me she seemed to have most of the qualities required by a dest-royer — speed, a fair gun and torpedo armament, and a reasonably inconspicuous silhouette. Compared with their contemporary destroyers, (the 'V' and 'W' class), the 'S' class were faster and less expensive to build, and far more rapidly turned out. Some of them were completed in six months. I was to remember the *Seafire* and her qualities many years later when the then First Sea Lord asked for my views as to the best means of producing a rapid extension in our destroyer building programmes. The craft then produced were the well-known 'Hunt' class''.

It is ironical that twenty years after these sixty-odd destroyers were completed only ten remained in service. Had the other fifty been kept in good condition in reserve instead of being allowed to rust away until scrapping was inevitable there would have been no need for the signing away of our West Indian bases to the Americans in 1940. The 'S' class destroyers were far superior in every way imaginable to the rubbishy old four-stackers we received so gratefully at that time, although built at the same time as the 'S' class. This was one of the penalties of short-sightedness between the wars.

Sesame's badge depicts the key of the robber's cave in Ali Baba, to which the password was "Open Sesame". She was built by Denny and completed on the 30th December 1918. From March to October 1919 she was in reserve at Devonport; then she commissioned for service in Scottish waters and undertook a visit to Denmark.

The reason for the delay between the completion date and her first commission was probably due to the manning problems the Admiralty faced through the speed of demobilization which was giving rise to great difficulties in finding sufficient men even for the reduced peacetime fleet. Many of the 'S' class at this time were running with only two-thirds crews, which made living and working aboard them very trying. The effects of national economy were also to be felt in the size of the flotillas which were ultimately to reduce the number of ships in each from twenty to nine. Thus many brand-new vessels lay alongside the dockyards for years before putting to sea.

In the old days of wooden ships this had been quite common but it had been rare before the Great War for a steel warship not to commission on completion. There was the inevitable deterioration of the hull and the more vulnerable fittings which lack of use and care made more pronounced and in reality it was a false economy. Destroyers are frail craft at best with very thin hulls and the active life at most was only considered to be fifteen years.

It is perhaps an indication of the soundness of British shipbuilding that some of *Sesame's* sister ships actually served in the Navy for almost double that period, including at the end of their days, gruelling seatime spent in the North Atlantic on convoy escort duties, much overladen with extra equipment. It is more remarkable when one considers that these craft were designed to operate in the more sheltered waters of the North Sea.

In 1920 she was in service with the 4th Destroyer Flotilla, Atlantic Fleet, and paid a visit to Germany. In 1921 she was replaced by a 'W' class destroyer and went into reserve again at Portsmouth. She was commissioned for further service in a Local Defence flotilla and during the time of the Irish troubles in 1923-28 saw much service in that area. In 1929 she was engaged in fleet target service and in 1930-32 was active in the Mediterranean before she was sold for scrap in 1933. She had served for fifteen years which was the allotted life-span for destroyers but unfortunately although about thirty of her type were scrapped that year, the Government of the time limited their replacement to nine destroyers, later reduced to five. Small wonder that when war came six years later the need for destroyers was so acute.

Sesame was the only vessel to bear the name in the Royal Navy. Her motto was a delightful play on words being, *Cave!* 'Beware'.

H.M.S. Stormcloud

A sister ship to *Sesame* and completed around the same period. This was *Stormcloud*, built by Palmer, completed on 30th May 1919 and first commissioned in January 1920. Her badge design depicts the North Cone which is hoisted as a warning that a Northerly storm is imminent.

Stormcloud served in Home Waters throughout 1920-22 in the 4th Destroyer Flotilla with *Sesame*.

When in 1923 the *Stormcloud* finished her first commission she paid off into reserve for two years. In 1926 however she was brought forward for limited service on account of the Irish problem and was employed on anti gun-running duties and patrols. She went to the China Station from 1927 until 1931, when she was relieved by larger destroyers of the 'W' class.

On her return to England *Stormcloud* was put on the disposal list and was sold in 1934 after her fifteen year span was almost up.

The name was revived for a vessel of the 'Algerine' class of Fleet Minesweepers. These were 850 ton vessels with a length of 225 feet, a speed of sixteen knots and an armament of one 4-inch and 8 20mm guns with a complement of 85 men. They were most useful ships both for their designed role and as slow coastal escorts. Although the exact opposite of the fast, lithe and heavily armed destroyers, many of them were given destroyer names and *Stormcloud* was one of them.

She was built by Lobnitz and launched in February 1944 being commissioned in time to serve during the landings in the South of France, which is the sole battle honour carried by this name. *Stormcloud* went to the breakers yard in August 1959, being scrapped at Gateshead, and the name has now passed out of service.

The motto of *Stormcloud*, *Omnibus tempestatibus*, means 'In all weathers.'

H.M.S. Telemachus

The naming of warships after characters in Greek and Roman mythology was very popular during the 18th century. It is said that the fourth Earl of Sandwich, who was First Lord of the Admiralty three times between 1748 and 1782 was responsible for this trend. The period saw the introduction into the service of names that have since made their own naval traditions to add to those of their mythical namesakes.

This name was that of the son of Ulysses and Penelope, both themselves much-used as ships names over the years and although a small vessel bore the name as early as 1795 it was the destroyer launched in April of 1917 by John Brown's shipyard that became the first major warship to adopt it. She was one of the very large War Emergency Programme of destroyers ordered on the 5th March 1916 to the Admiralty 'R' class design. They displaced just over 1,000 tons and carried three 4-inch guns and four torpedo-tubes and cost approximately £167,000 each.

Telemachus herself was typical of the hundreds of destroyers which joined the fleet during the Great War but was to have an added interest for students of naval history for her commander was Captain Taprell Dorling, D.S.O., known better to generations of historians and lovers of the sea and ships as 'Taffrail'. In between long and exhausting periods in command of destroyers during the war he wrote scores of articles and several best-selling books, which brought home to the public, starved as they were by the wartime censorship of news of the fleet, exactly what life and conditions were for those at sea. After the war he continued in command of destroyers for a time and produced several small ships histories which have stood the test of time as classics of their sort.

When *Telemachus* first commissioned it was to work with the fleet in a normal destroyer function, but in January 1917 it was proposed that some destroyers should be fitted as fast minelayers. The war had found Britain deficient in vessels of this type which had the speed to dash into hostile waters at night, deposit their mines and be clear by dawn. The destroyer proved the ideal ship for the task. *Telemachus* and her sister ship, *Tarpon*, were therefore adapted for this duty. Within a short time of reaching harbour from a conventional patrol they could land their after guns and embark mines, forty in all, minerails and sinkers and be ready for their new operations within forty-eight hours.

During 1917-18 these ships and the other destroyers that were converted later, were formed into the specialised 20th Minelaying Flotilla and their duties were to lay their mines inside the enemy's swept channels. To penetrate German minefields by night, lay their own mines inside, and then get free took a very special form of courage and not surprisingly casualties were heavy but *Telemachus* survived, and also saw service with the Dover patrol. After the war she went into reserve and was finally scrapped in 1926.

The name was handed on in 1942 when the 'T' class submarine *P.321* was building at the Barrow yard of Vickers Armstrong. This was the result of an interesting sidelight on the importance of names even to the modern seamen of World War II. Before the war all submarines had been given names like any other warship, but after 1939 it was decided to revert to the old First World War practice of giving them numbers only in order to mislead the enemy on the numbers being built and the classes under construction.

This proved highly unpopular in the submarine service and the crews very soon began to adopt their own names for their ships instead of the dreary Initial letter and three numbers they were allocated. Some of these names, as may be imagined, were hardly in the naval tradition! In 1942 the Prime Minister, Winston Churchill got to hear of this and mindful of the poor effect on morale this policy was having he directed that all the submarines were to be named at once, and so they were. Thus *P.321* became *Telemachus* before she sailed for the Indian Ocean to seek out Japanese shipping off the coast of Malaya and occupied Burma.

She was of 1,090 tons surface displacement, carried a crew of 65 and was armed with a single 4-inch gun and eleven 21-inch torpedoes. Despite the circumstances under which they were forced to operate from their base in Ceylon these submarines were most successful. To the normal far from pleasant conditions always associated with submarines were added the climatic conditions of the Indian Ocean for which these submarines had not been specifically designed. Indeed on one occasion a submarine signalled back to base the readings of humidity during a patrol and received back the signal from Flag Officer, Submarines: —

'The figures you report will not support life'.

Nevertheless the 'T' boats struck the Japanese hard and *Telemachus* contributed her share to their ultimate defeat when, under the command of Commander William King she sank the large Japanese transport submarine *I.166* in the Malacca Straits on 17th July 1944. *Telemachus* survived the war and remained in the Far East, seeing service as one of the only British submarines on that station during the Korean War in 1953. With the coming of the nuclear-powered submarine she had obviously had her day and was finally brought home and sold. She was scrapped at Charlestown during August 1961 after a life-span of almost twenty years, which is very long for a submarine.

The badge design is that of a dolphin, gold, and the motto, *Per me tutus*, means 'Safe through me'. This is a reference to the fact that Telemachus was saved from drowning by a dolphin.

H.M.S. Valhalla

Valhalla is the Hall of Odin, in Norse mythology, to which the souls of heroes who die in action are transported for eternal revel and feasting. The warship which was given this name was a flotilla leader built during the Great War.

Destroyers were a weapon to be used in mass, and were therefore organised accordingly in groups of twenty vessels, the flotilla system. To exercise control over such a large number of high speed small craft the Captain (D), the senior officer in command of the whole flotilla, had before the war been housed, with his staff, in a fast light cruiser which provided the extra space and specialist equipment. However as developments during the period 1913-17 had led to ever increasing speeds of destroyers it was decided that light cruisers were no longer really suitable craft for this job and a specially enlarged destroyer took her place, the flotilla leader.

With the production of the 'R' class destroyers of 1916-17, as *Telemachus*, already described, even higher average speeds were expected and following requests from sea the Admiralty considered the construction of a new type of leader to fill the bill. The first three when laid down were named *Malcolm*, *Montrose*, and *Wallace* after Scottish Clans but before completion their design, although a great advance on that which had gone before, had already been overtaken and the ships were subsequently re-classified as 'half-leaders' and renamed according to the well established alphabetical system which by this time had reached the letter V. They became *Valorous*, *Vampire* and *Valkyrie* and when the two additional ships were ordered from Cammell Laird's shipyard they were named in the *Va* tradition as *Valentine* and *Valhalla*.

They presented a new concept in destroyer design when they joined the fleet and for the first time the main armament was in two sets of single guns super-firing ahead and astern whereas before the arrangement had been for the midships gun to be sighted between the funnels, a wasteful location which had restricted the firing arcs of the weapon.

Valhalla was 309 feet long on the waterline with a beam of 29½ feet and a standard displacement of 1,188 tons. She was powered by Parsons geared turbines which developed a S.H.P. of 27,000 driving her through the water at 34 knots. She had a complement of 115 officers and men and was powerfully armed with four 4-inch guns, a 3-inch AA gun and four torpedo tubes in two twin mountings.

Valhalla was twin screwed, her boilers were of the Yarrow type of which she was fitted with three and she had a bunkerage for 367 tons of oil fuel which gave her a radius of action of 3500 nautical miles at her most economical speed, fifteen knots.

With their new layout of gun armament with two guns super-imposed both fore and aft these destroyers set a standard which lasted twenty years and were well liked in the service for their comfort and reliability. Most surprising was the fact that at a total cost of around £218,300, they worked out cheaper than earlier flotilla leaders yet were vastly superior in all respects. Toward the end of the war the twin sets of double torpedo tubes were replaced by triple thus bringing them into line with their later sisters.

Although built as leaders for the standard destroyer flotillas their successful design was utilised when it was decided, later in the war, to build large numbers of these bigger destroyers in reply to equally larger ships being built by the Germans. The five 'Va' ships therefore became the prototypes of the famous 'V' & 'W' destroyers which served the fleet for over thirty years in two World Wars.

Valhalla herself was completed in late 1917 and joined the fleet in time for the last year of the war in which time she saw much hard service. Half-leaders continued to be utilised, the newly formed 3rd Flotilla, for example, being led by *Campbell* with *Valhalla* as half-leader. The flotillas still numbered over twenty ships, but in 1921 there was a reorganisation on economy grounds and they were reduced to one leader and eight destroyers. The need for the half-leader having passed, *Valhalla* was de-rated to ordinary destroyer but, with her extra spacious internal fittings, was much in demand by the senior officers.

The average life span of a destroyer had been agreed as twelve years by the Washington Naval Conference, but due again to economy the Admiralty extended this to fifteen or sixteen years. In January 1930 *Valhalla* and her sisters, now approaching the twelve year limit, still formed the whole of the front-line destroyer strength of the Royal Navy. During prolonged manouvres off Cape St. Vincent the 5th and 6th flotillas ran into a south-easterly gale on 19th January of that year and despite constant reductions of speed down to twelve knots a great number of the 'V's and 'W's. including *Valhalla*, were soon in difficulties. No less than four had serious leaks and *Valhalla* had to be docked in Gibraltar on her return.

This probably hastened her demise, for she was the first of her class to go to the breakers yard, being sold in December 1931 and broken up the following year. What is surprising is not that she was scrapped when she was but the fact that over fifty of her sister ships continued to serve right through until 1945.

Since *Valhalla* was broken up the name has been revived briefly in the service but not for a fighting vessel. *Valhalla* was the name of a yacht taken over during World War II and used as an accommodation ship. Thus the name carries no battle honours. The badge shows a star, silver, encircled by a wreath of gold. The motto *Mors janua vitae* means, 'Death is the gate of life'.

Part Two

Boat Badges

Action against German submarines in World War One. From the painting 'Clearing the Seas!' by C.E. Turner at the Imperial War Museum. (Copyright I.W.M.).

H.M.S. Amazon

The name is derived from the legendary tribe of warrior women who fought against the Greek Heroes and hence the badge features the stern, helmeted features of a martial female. It was obviously most suitable for the name of a warship, which can also be described as a fighting female, and no less than ten ships of the Royal Navy have carried the name over two centuries.

The first was the French *Panthère* taken as a prize in 1745 and renamed. As *Amazon* she served the fleet until 1763 when she was sold out of service. The second vessel to receive this name was also a prize ship, *Subtile* taken in 1746, but the first ship to be built for the Royal Navy as *Amazon* was a frigate launched in 1773. She saw twenty years service before being broken up in 1794.

Almost immediately the name was passed on to another frigate built in 1795 but she had a very brief and tragic lifespan for she was wrecked in 1797.

The fifth *Amazon* was likewise a frigate which joined the Navy in 1799. Her war service included the battle of Copenhagen in 1801 when the British fleet, under Sir Hyde Parker, with Nelson as second-in-command, smashed decisively the Danish fleet and thus prevented it adding its considerable strength to the maritime power of Napoleon. The fifth *Amazon* was sold in 1812.

A 5th-rate next bore the name in 1821 and served until 1863 before being sold and her place was taken in the Victorian Navy by the sloop *Amazon* of 1865. Like the third ship of the name her days were short for she was lost in a collision the following year.

It was not until forty years later that the name was revived after being considered unlucky. The eighth ship of the name was one of the very large destroyers of the 'Ocean' class which took to the water during Admiral Fisher's forceful period in the early 1900's.

Designed to obtain the maximum of speed, the armaments provided were pathetically inadequate for their size. Fisher was determined not to hamper his greyhounds with heavy guns and accordingly *Amazon* carried only two 4-inch guns and two torpedo tubes on a displacement of 970 tons.

Amazon was built by Thornycroft and was launched in 1908. Although termed 'Oceans', this quickly proved to be a misnomer for their range was short and they were really only suitable for coastal operations. Nor were the sensational speeds attributed to them accurate, *Amazon* herself being credited with 33 knots at best. Fisher is thought to have designed these large vessels to replace small cruisers and to use them to block the exits of the North Sea to prevent the use of German commerce raiders. Their names included some tribes such as the *Tartar, Maori* and *Mohawk* and so they quickly became popularly known in the fleet as the 'Tribals'. Although this was hardly accurate in all cases it caught the public imagination.

Although they proved unsuitable for the role they were built for and were uneconomical and poorly armed, their wartime exploits soon earned them an honoured place in naval history. Old when the Great War commenced they were nevertheless extremely active with Admiral Bacon's immortal Dover Patrol. Here they were constantly in action and suffered losses, but *Amazon* survived the war intact and was sold in 1919.

There was a ten year holiday from destroyer construction following the Great War but when the Admiralty finally proceeded with a modest programme of new construction they placed the orders for two prototypes with the foremost destroyer builders of the day, Yarrow and Thornycroft. Thus is was that the ninth *Amazon*, like the eighth, was built by this firm. She displaced 1,170 tons, had a length of 312 feet and was built for a speed of 37 knots. Her main armament consisted of four 4.7-inch guns and six 21-inch torpedo tubes and when she took to the water in 1926 there were the same cries that she was too large as had greeted her predecessor. Nevertheless her design was most successful and after a long proving cruise to South America *Amazon* and her sister the *Ambuscade*, were the design on which all subsequent destroyer building for the next decade was based.

Both were brought out of reserve on the outbreak of the Second World War and both had long and distinguished war records. *Amazon* herself served in the front line during the campaign off Norway in 1940 and was later converted to an escort destroyer role with increased anti-submarine capability. In this new guise she served in the Atlantic from 1939-43 with sorties into the even more dangerous fields of the Arctic and Malta Convoys in 1942. She was also present during the landings in North Africa in November of that year and was credited with the destruction of a German submarine but this was not subsequently confirmed post-war.

By 1943 they had become too old for these duties and they finished the war as anti-submarine training vessels and later as aircraft target vessels, *Amazon* herself being finally scrapped at Troon in October 1948 after twenty years service.

The latest *Amazon* to join the fleet is another prototype for a new class of small vessel, being the name ship of the Type 21 frigates now being built for the Royal Navy. This class is designed as an interim frigate of 2,040 tons by Messrs. Yarrows and Vospers. They are powered by gas turbines and have a new automatic rapid fire 4.5-inch gun, a Seacat missile system and a Lynx helicopter. *Amazon*, launched in April 1971, is now serving with the fleet and is to be joined by her sisters *Active* and *Antelope*.

The ship's motto is *Audacater* 'Boldly'.

H.M.S. Amphion

Amphion was a king of Thebes, noted for his outstanding skill as a musician. The first *Amphion* in the Royal Navy was a 5th rate which was launched in 1780 at a time when the naming of warships with classical names was at its height. She saw sixteen years service and was blown up in 1796. The second *Amphion* took to the water in 1798. Also a 5th-rate, she joined the Mediterranean Fleet and saw action in the Adriatic in 1809 against France's Neapolitan allies and two years later she was with Captain William Hoste's squadron which defeated a combined French and allied fleet at the battle of Lissa. The second *Amphion* continued to serve well into the long peace, being sold in 1823.

Yet another 5th-rate to adopt the name *Amphion* was launched in 1846 and she also managed to see action, this time with the Baltic Fleet during the Crimea War under the command of Admiral Dundas, during the years 1854-55. She was sold out of service in 1863.

The old rating system had ended before the next *Amphion* took to the water. She was a cruiser built in 1883 and she survived until 1906 without seeing any major action in her long service. The name was now established as a cruiser name and in 1910 the name was allocated to a new fast light cruiser building at Pembroke Dockyard. She was listed as a 'Scout', which was a new type of fast, lightly armed cruiser.

It must be remembered that the destroyers of this period had neither the space nor the freeboard to make satisfactory control of a flotilla practical. Under the flotilla system twenty destroyers had to be handled and controlled as a single unit in order to synchronise massed attacks. The volume of smoke generated by this number of small craft at full speed in the misty conditions so prevalent in the North Sea made the signalling necessary for such tight control most difficult and the low freeboard of the destroyer added to this problem.

The necessary staff of specialist officers needed to organise and operate this large number of vessels was far too great to be accommodated in a destroyer whose bridge was only a slight improvement on the canvas screen around the forward gun that had served the earliest ships of this type. Therefore although the paper speed of the light cruiser was never as high as a destroyer they could, in any sort of seaway keep up and so retain control, although this proved more difficult later when speeds of destroyers continued to rise and their weather qualities also improved. Furthermore the 6-inch guns of the light cruiser would always provide valuable support for the destroyers if hard pressed.

This graceful little craft displaced only 3,440 tons and carried an armament of ten 4-inch guns and two 21-inch torpedo tubes and had a complement of 330 men and a speed of 26 knots. She was completed in 1912 and two years later, on the outbreak of war, was with her flotilla, the 3rd, which consisted of twenty of the brand-new 'L' class destroyers based at Harwich. The Harwich Force was commanded by Commodore Reginald Tyrwhitt and *Amphion* was commanded by Captain C. H. Fox.

It was to *Amphion's* flotilla that the honour of firing the first British shots of World War One was given. They were on the first sweep into the North Sea after the declaration of war when they sighted and quickly overhauled the German minelayer *Konigin Luise* which had been busy sowing mines off their base early on the 5th August 1914. The destroyer *Lance* commenced firing, and soon after *Amphion*, rated as one of the best shooting ships of her class in the Navy, also came within range and quickly reduced the German vessel to a shambles.

Survivors were picked up but on the return to Harwich *Amphion* herself fell victim to one of the mines, as at 6.45 a.m. an explosion took place under her bridge which set fire to the cordite in the forward magazines. There were heavy casualties among her forward gun crews and bridge personnel but she was still moving through the water when she hit a second mine and sank with the loss of 147 of her crew and all the German prisoners.

The sixth *Amphion* was a light cruiser also, being of the Improved 'Leander' Class, launched in July 1934. She displaced 6,980 tons and carried eight 6-inch and eight 4-inch guns and eight 21-inch torpedo tubes. On completion however she was handed over to the Australian Navy and never served in the Royal Navy. She was re-named *Perth* and after service in the Mediterranean she was sunk by Japanese cruisers and destroyers during the invasion of Java in 1942.

The name then broke with tradition with its allocation to an 'A' class submarine launched by Vickers Armstrong of Barrow in August 1944. These were somewhat larger than the normal submarines of the time and were designed for operations against the Japanese in Far Eastern waters. They featured a higher surface speed and greater endurance and were of pre-fabricated and all welded construction to speed delivery. Large numbers were ordered and laid down but the war against Japan ended before any could be used operationally.

Many of those building were cancelled but *Amphion* and her sisters were too far advanced and were completed. They formed the backbone of British submarine strength for more than fifteen years before being replaced in the early 1960's by the conventional boats of the *Porpoise* and *Oberon* classes. A few still survive in the fleet today much modernised, but *Amphion* herself was broken up in 1968.

The design of the badge shows a dragon's head, green, out of a Naval Crown, gold. The motto is 'Fear None'.

H.M.S. Boreas

Boreas is the God of the North Wind and the badge depicts him blowing a storm with great energy. The first ship to carry the name was a 6th-rate launched in 1757. She soon saw active service for her first duty was service with the fleet assembling on Pitt's orders, during the Seven Years' War, to capture Louisburg in French Canada.

Accordingly a powerful squadron was assembled at Halifax, Nova Scotia under the able command of Admiral Boscawen. The French garrison was under a blockade already and an army commanded by Major-General Amherst, with a certain Brigadier James Wolfe as second in command, was also despatched. *Boreas* joined the main fleet which assembled during May in readiness for the assault. A French squadron had meantime taken advantage of the bad weather to break through to the garrisons of Louisburg and Quebec which meant that the French were now well supplied.

Boscawen was determined to give them no further time in which to consolidate and he quickly assembled his great fleet and transports with the troops aboard and on the morning of June 8th 1758 the assault went in by the ships' boats. They were met by a determined defence but eventually the troops under Wolfe got ashore, repulsed a French counter-attack and moved on to take the defences of the town. While the troops constructed trenches around the French garrison the fleet continued to blockade and bombard. For the rest of the month the French gradually lost more and more of their ships in the harbour and the dashing Wolfe succeeded in outflanking the garrison. Finally an attack by the fleet's boats resulted in the loss of the last two French warships and the town and garrison of Louisburg surrendered on July 26th.

Boreas was again in the thick of the fighting further south along the American Continent when she took part in the last act of the Seven Years' War, the capture of Havana from Spain. *Boreas* continued to serve for some years after this crowning achievement and was finally sold in 1770.

The second ship of the name was also a 6th-rate launched in 1774, and although not sold until 1802 she saw no major action worthy of a battle honour. A sloop launched in 1806 wore the name for less than a year before being wrecked in 1807 and it was not until 120 years later that a major fighting vessel was again named *Boreas*. She was a destroyer built by Palmers and launched in 1930. She had a displacement of 1,360 tons, an armament of four 4.7-inch guns and eight 21-inch torpedo tubes. The ships of this class all had an overall length of 323 feet and the deep displacement of *Boreas* was 1,792 tons. She cost £221,156. They were powered by Parsons turbines and fitted with three Admiralty 3-drum type boilers which developed 300 lbs-per-square-inch pressure. On her six hour trial the *Boreas*, with a S.H.P. of 35,398 attained a speed of 35.78 knots. She was typical of the destroyers of this period which although presenting a graceful and pleasing appearance always gave the impression of being under-gunned compared with rival ships abroad. In fact the lighter 4.7-inch gun was a highly reliable weapon with a good rate of fire and as sea boats they were unexcelled anywhere in the world. At the time that these destroyers were building, foreign destroyer types were undergoing radical changes. The Italians had announced some trial figures which showed that their new destroyers were exceeding 40-knots with ease. Against this *Boreas* could only show 35¾-knots on her trials and there was some disappointment in this. But although it was at one time proposed that a 'special' trial be held which would equal foreign figures the firms consulted were not very enthusiastic for many felt that these figures would be meaningless.

The Japanese had begun to fit their destroyers with the new 5-inch gun they had developed. It was capable of firing at a high elevation and could therefore tackle both air and surface targets. British designers could not make a satisfactory reply to this. The new Japanese weapon was capable of firing at 70-degrees elevation, whereas the British ships guns had a maximum elevation of only 30-degrees. Furthermore the gun crews were out in the open whereas the Japanese mounted their guns in turrets to give some weather protection.

Other considerations weighed with the British designers however and the 'B' class was fitted with extra depth charges and one shipped an improved asdic dome. This was an echo sounding device used to locate submarines and was an indication that the Admiralty was taking the threat of the submarine quite seriously. Although Germany was at this time banned from building, Italy and Japan had large numbers on hand. On her completion in 1932 she served with the Mediterranean Fleet in the 2nd Flotilla and then went into reserve until the outbreak of World War Two.

During the summer of 1940 the destroyers of the 'B' class formed the 4th Flotilla operating in the English Channel and several were lost during the Dunkirk evacuation and the subsequent dive-bombing of the Channel ports and convoys in July, *Boreas* herself being damaged at this time.

After repairs she served in the South Atlantic during 1941 and 1942 then took part in the North African landings and served in the Mediterranean in 1942-43. In that year she was loaned to the Greek Navy and renamed *Salamis*. She remained until 1952 a unit of the Greek Navy and on her return to the Royal Navy in that year she was immediately sold and scrapped at Troon in April. Since that time the name has passed out of the service.

The motto of *Boreas*, is *Vento favente*, 'With fair winds'.

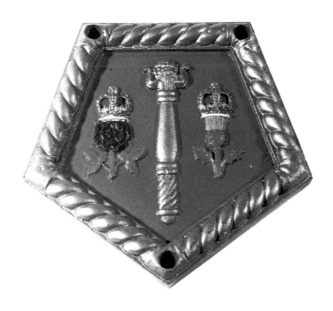

H.M.S. Caroline

The first vessel of this name was named after the consort of George IV, hence the design of the badge. A 5th rate launched in 1795, she went out to the East Indies and took part in the actions off Java in both 1807 and 1811 and the action of Banda Neira in 1810. She came home and was broken up in 1815.

The name was an extremely popular one in the service and was borne by a succession of small craft during Victoria's reign including a Crimea gunboat in 1855 but the next major vessel was a corvette of 1882 which was to become *Ganges* in 1908 as part of that well-known training establishment at Shotley.

The sixth and final *Caroline* was a light cruiser which gave her name to a class of six vessels which were completed in the early years of the Great War. She displaced 3,750 tons, had a length of 446 feet and a beam of 41½ feet. She carried an armament of four 6-inch and two 3-inch guns and four 21-inch torpedo tubes. She had a complement of 325 officers and men and was capable of a speed of 30 knots.

She was built by the firm of Cammell Laird who completed her for service in the remarkable time of eleven months.

Caroline herself joined the Grand Fleet and was present at the Battle of Jutland and under the command of Captain Crooke made a lone and very gallant attack on the German battle-fleet towards the end of that engagement. She ended the war and remained with the fleet until 1926 when she was refitted and taken to Belfast where she became the Royal Naval Volunteer Reserve Drill Ship. When her usefulness eventually comes to an end the Maritime Trust hope to preserve her as an example of the only Jutland warship still afloat today.

The badge design features a sceptre, gold, between a crowned rose and thistle proper. The sceptre is from the Arms of Brandenberg. The ship's motto is *Tenax propositi* 'Firm of purpose'.

H.M.S. Castor

The name is derived from the legend of Castor, one of the Dioscuri, or the Heavenly Twins, the sons of Leda by the god Zeus. A French vessel of 36 guns was the first ship to carry this name in the Royal Navy when she was taken as a prize in 1781.

The second ship named *Castor* was a 5th rate built in 1785 and she fought Napoleon's fleet in the Mediterranean at Toulon in 1793 and later in the West Indies at the actions of San Sebastian in 1807, Martinique in 1808 and Guadeloupe in 1810 with some distinction. She was finally sold out in 1819 after a very active life span.

Her replacement was another 5th rate launched in 1832 and she too added lustre to the name of *Castor*. She was present during the Syrian campaign of 1840 and later went out to the Pacific station where she fought in the wars against the Maoris in New Zealand in 1845-47. Although long past her usefulness towards the end of the 19th century she was not sold out of the Navy until 1902.

The name passed to a small vessel and then in 1915 was given to a light cruiser, sister ship to *Caroline*, completed in 1915 but belonging to a different group which could be identified by having two funnels instead of three. Her armament and other details were the same. *Castor* became famous as the leader of the Grand Fleet destroyer flotillas during the Great War, flying throughout the pennant of Commodore (F) Grand Fleet Flotillas. In this capacity she was also present at the battle of Jutland under Commodore Hawksley, and led the 11th Flotilla against the German battleships early in the main action. She survived this tough action and continued to serve with the Grand Fleet in the North Sea until 1918.

She served for several years in the post-war fleet on overseas stations before being sold in 1935.

Castor's badge shows a horse's head, white, caparisoned red, for Castor was famed as a horse tamer. The motto *Frenavimus mare* means, 'We have tamed the sea'.

H.M.S. Danae

Danae was, in classical history, the daughter of Acrisius, King of Argos, and mother of Perseus. It was the name of a 5th rate taken as a prize in 1759 and not broken up until 1771. This was also the case with the second *Danae*, a 5th rate taken as prize in 1779. She served the Royal Navy until 1797 before being sold.

The third ship of the name was another prize and another 5th rate, the French *Vaillante*, taken in 1798 and renamed. She hardly reflected the honour of the service however and scarcely covered herself with glory for the crew mutinied in 1800 and took *Danae* back to her former owners at Brest.

Understandably therefore some sixty-five years were to pass before the name was again considered suitable for one of Her Majesty's ships. This, the fourth *Danae*, was a Victorian corvette launched in 1867. After a long and undistinguished life she was finally sold in 1905.

In 1918, *Danae* was the nameship of a new enlarged class of light cruiser. She had a tonnage of 4,650 tons and an armament of six single 6-inch guns and two 3-inch AA guns, with a heavy torpedo armament of twelve 21-inch. She carried a crew of 400 and was capable of a speed of 29 knots.

The *Danae* had an overall length of 471 feet and a beam of 46 feet. She had geared turbines which developed 40,000 s.h.p. and had twin screws. Her armour, as was the case with all light cruisers of this type, was thin and she carried only a 3-inch thick belt with 1-inch decks. She was of course not built for the battle-line and her duties were more akin to the destroyers work than the battle-cruisers. *Danae* and her sisters were developed especially to work with the destroyer flotillas and had to be light and fast enough to do so. In certain circumstances they would also form a light screen ahead of the battle fleet, like the frigates of Nelson's day, to bring the first word of the enemy strength and dispositions, but it was not their task to stand and fight it out, merely to report. None the less they were equipped with 6-inch guns so that they could provide heavy enough fire to break up any attempt by enemy destroyer flotillas to mount an attack of the normal sort with torpedoes against the head of the British battle fleet.

Nor was she designed to fulfil the other function associated with the cruiser type, that of patrolling the sea lanes in the more distant oceans. She had neither the endurance nor the size for this. The *Danae* and her sisters were really built for the waters of the North Sea only and as such were valuable additions to the Harwich Force and the Grand Fleet. Although they were used extensively abroad during the peace they were not the ideal ships for foreign stations, being small and cramped.

Life aboard the *Danae* was no sinecure as witness an account of a voyage in one of her sister ships in 1927.

"Her stern wagged up and down about four feet, and made one wonder when it might break off. We struggled on when the weather moderated and passed the Azores on Christmas Day, having, as we thought, lashed and secured everything on the upper deck. Two days later we ran into another howling gale from the northward. This brought the wind and sea right abeam and various fittings on the upper deck was smashed or washed overboard". *

Built by Armstrong Whitworth, she joined the Harwich Force for the closing stages of the war, in the 5th Light Cruiser Squadron.

She remained in service between the wars and in 1939 was serving on the China Station where she remained until 1941. She had a lucky escape from destruction when the Japanese Navy annihilated the Allied surface fleet during the invasion of Java in 1942 and for a time served with the East Indies Fleet. She returned home in 1944 and was lent to the free Polish Navy who renamed her *Conrad* after their most famous maritime author. As such she was present in a bombarding role during the Normandy landings and remained with the Home Fleet for the rest of the war. She was handed back to the Royal Navy in 1946 and two years later was scrapped at Barrow.

The name was then allocated to one of the big 'Daring' class destroyers then under construction, but post-war economies led to her cancellation before launch. The sixth and present bearer of the name *Danae* is one of the modern 'Leander' class frigates. Equipped to perform a general purpose role and replacing both the cruiser and destroyer as well as the old type escort frigates, they are armed with a twin 4.5 inch gun turret, Seacat anti-aircraft missiles, and a Wasp helicopter armed with homing missiles. *Danae* was launched in 1965 and has a displacement of 2,200 tons, a length of 370 feet and carries a crew of 260 officers and men.

The *Danae* of mythology was confined by her father in a tower of brass and was visited there by Jupiter in a shower of gold, hence the design of the badge which shows a castle, gold. The motto *Timeant Danaeios* means, 'Let them fear those belonging to Danae'.

---

* From *A Sailor's Odyssey*, Viscount Cunningham of Hyndhope, Hutchinson, 1951.

H.M.S. Dauntless

The first ship to be named *Dauntless* was a sloop constructed in 1804 but in spite of the name her end came a mere three years later in surrender. She was quickly replaced by another sloop of the same name which remained with the fleet until 1825.

Dauntless of 1847 was a frigate and she it was who established the name in the annals of the Navy. She saw service during the Crimea War both in the Baltic squadron in 1854 and in the Black Sea a year later.

The fourth *Dauntless* was a light cruiser launched in 1918 and a sister ship of *Danae*, and it is her boat badge which we illustrate here. Like *Danae* she joined the 5th Light Cruiser Squadron at Harwich after completion by Palmer's shipyard. After a short period of war service she joined the post-war fleet and served as a flagship on the various overseas stations, taking turns with her sister ships.

In 1928 she went out to the American and West Indies Station and it was here that her story almost reached a premature conclusion. She ran aground off Halifax, Nova Scotia on July 2nd in heavy seas.

The recovery operation, however, was successful, for after her armament was removed her sister ship *Despatch* pulled her off the rocks and she was subsequently repaired.

She later served in the 3rd Light Cruiser Squadron with the Mediterranean Fleet in 1935 during the confrontation with Italy over the invasion of Abyssinia. She served through the Second World War in the same capacity as *Danae*, in the Far East and in the East Indies and then returned home to become a training ship in 1943-45. She was scrapped at Inverkeithing in February 1946.

The name *Dauntless* however remained in the Navy as it became the identification of the W.R.N.S. Depot at Burghfield, Reading from 1947.

The design of the badge shows the head of Horatius, who kept the bridge, wearing a helmet, gold, arising out of wavelets, green and silver. Her motto is *Nil desperandum*, 'Never despair'.

H.M.S. Devonshire

The badge is derived from the arms of Devonshire, as is the motto, *Auxilio Divino* 'By the help of God' and is a very ancient name in the Royal Navy. However it is quite likely that the first ship was so named, not from the county, but after William Cavendish, Earl (later Duke) of Devonshire who was a prominent supporter of William III.

She was a 2nd rate of 1,220 tons launched at Bursledon in 1692 and she carried eight guns. In her first year of service she saw action at the battles of Cape Barfleur and La Hogue while in 1697 she was present at Harlow's action against de Pointis, being rebuilt at Woolwich in 1704. On 10th October 1707 she was in Commodore Edwards' squadron during the engagement with the French Admiral Trouin. *Devonshire* was hard pressed by no less than five of the enemy in a running engagement that lasted until dusk. She was finally overwhelmed and blew up in action with the loss of all her crew save two.

Such a gallant struggle did not long pass unrecorded and the second vessel to carry the name *Devonshire* was a 3rd rate with 80 guns, constructed at Woolwich in December 1710. Her first duty was to provide escort to a provision convoy in support of Rear-Admiral Hovenden Walker's expedition to Quebec. In 1717 she went out to the Baltic and in 1740 she was hulked at Woolwich, finally being broken up twenty years later.

Meanwhile a third *Devonshire*, another 3rd rate, had replaced her in the active fleet. Displacing 1,470 tons she carried 66 guns in service although launched as an 80 gun vessel in 1745. At the battle of Finisterre in 1747 she served under Anson with distinction, capturing the French *Serieux* which was flying the flag of the French Admiral de la Jonquiere. Later the same year, while serving as the flagship of Admiral Hawke, she took part in the battle of Ushant during which she captured the French *Terrible* and succeeded in forcing two others to surrender.

She later served in Admiral Saunders' fleet which so ably supported General

Wolfe in the capture of Quebec in 1759, and was present at the capture, the following year, of Montreal. The destruction of the French Empire in the Americas continued apace and the British fleet invested the West Indies, *Devonshire* being at the capture of both Martinique and Havana in 1762. This famous vessel was finally scrapped at Portsmouth in 1772. She was certainly the best known of *Devonshire's* but she has been followed by others.

The fourth was a small ship of which details are lacking while the fifth was a 3rd rate built on the Thames in 1812. She was 1,742 tons and carried 74 guns and although she joined the fleet towards the end of the Napoleonic wars she saw no major action. She was utilised for a short time as a hospital ship at Greenwich in 1849 and in 1854 became a prison hulk at Sheerness during the Crimea War. She finished her days as a school vessel, being broken up at Sheerness in 1869.

It was not until 1904 that another *Devonshire* joined the Royal Navy and she was the largest of them all, being one of the 'County' class of armoured cruisers. She displaced 10,850 tons and was built by Chatham Dockyard in 1904. She had a length of 475 feet and was driven by triple expansion engines at 22 knots. Mounting four 7.5 inch guns, six 6-inch guns and two 12-pdrs, she also carried two 18-inch torpedo tubes and had a complement of 700 men. The Armoured Cruiser was a type that was steadily developed during the years 1900 to 1907 until they reached a size and power equivalent to a second-class battleship. They were designed for convoy route protection in distant waters and were finally surpassed by the Battle-Cruiser design introduced with *Invincible*.

Devonshire herself served with the 3rd Cruiser Squadron of the Grand Fleet and was present at the battles of Heligoland and Dogger Bank in 1914 and 1915. In 1916 she went out to the North America and West Indies Station and ended her days when she was sold to shipbreakers.

The Washington Treaty limited ships of the heavy cruiser type to 10,000 tons and 8-inch guns, and it was to this specification that the seventh *Devonshire* was laid down for a new 'County' class. She was built by Devonport Dockyard and launched in October 1927. On a displacement of 9,850 tons she carried eight 8-inch guns and eight 4-inch guns and an aircraft of the amphibious type which she launched by means of a catapult. She had a crew of 650 and in the early thirties joined the First Cruiser Squadron of the Mediterranean Fleet under Admiral Sir William Fisher based at Malta and remained there until 1939 when she was serving as the flagship of Rear-Admiral J. H. D. Cunningham.

She returned home later that year and joined the Home Fleet where she remained until 1942. Then she was sent to join the Eastern Fleet under Admiral Somerville in the Indian Ocean. In 1943 she returned to the Home Fleet and was one of the cruisers which escorted *Queen Mary* at 29 knots when she crossed the North Atlantic with Winston Churchill aboard. She saw out her days in wartime on the Home Station. She served in the training capacity from 1947 until 1953 and was finally scrapped at Newport in 1955.

The name has been perpetuated in yet another 'County' class however. This is *Devonshire* at present serving with the fleet. She is a 5,200 ton guided-missile destroyer and carries a *Seaslug* long-range missile system, *Seacat* close-range missiles and four 4.5-inch guns for surface actions. She was built in 1960 and although thirteen years old is still one of the most powerful surface warships in the Navy today.

H.M.S. Eclipse

The design of the badge is accompanied by the motto 'None shall eclipse me'. *Eclipse* was a very popular small ship name from 1715 onward and the early battle honours feature such far flung campaigns as Mauritius in 1810, New Zealand in 1863-64 and Suez in 1882. The ship which earned Suez honour was a sloop built in 1867 which later became a mine depot.

The first major ship to carry the name *Eclipse* was a protected cruiser which was the lead ship of a class built in 1896-99. Cruisers as a distinct type of warship appeared in the 1880's and were divided into two categories, the armoured cruiser and the protected cruiser. The protected cruisers were built without side armour, but with armoured decks to protect their vitals and a distribution of coal bunkerage to provide some side protection. The armoured cruiser relied on side armour. Both types became obsolete tonnage by the time of the Great War, and were later replaced by heavy and light cruisers whose main difference lay in the calibre of guns carried.

Eclipse and her sisters displaced some 5,600 tons, were 370 feet long and had a crew of 450. They were capable of a speed of 19½ knots and had an armament of eleven 6-inch guns and three 18-inch torpedo tubes. *Eclipse* herself was built by Pembroke Dockyard, and although nearly obsolete in 1914 she served in the 12th Cruiser Squadron on the Western Channel Patrol. In 1916 she became a depot ship and after the war she was sold.

The tenth and last *Eclipse* was a 1,375 ton destroyer built by Denny and launched in April 1934. She carried four single 4.7-inch guns and eight 21-inch torpedo tubes at a speed of 36 knots and had a crew of 145.

Eclipse was 329 feet overall with a beam of 33¼ feet. She was fitted with an asdic dome for the detection of submarines and carried twenty depth-charges. Her engines were Parsons geared turbines developing 36,000 S.H.P. and she had the standard Admiralty 3-drum type boilers. She was a very fast ship and on her official speed trials touched 37½ knots.

The destroyers of the 'E' class were all designed so that their main armament of 4.7-inch guns could elevate to 40-degrees. This reflected the growing concern in the fleet that our modern destroyers were almost totally impotent in the face of air attack. The arguments put forward at the time were that as the main function of the destroyer was to screen the battle fleet, there was no need for them to carry anti-aircraft weapons for they themselves would be protected from bombing by the heavy A.A. guns of the battleships. As it was, the guns mounted in the *Eclipse* could only elevate to 40-degrees through a clumsy arrangement of removable deck plates.

The whole class was originally to be designed so that they could operate as fast minelayers. Difficulties in evaluation of their potential however resulted in only two being so designed, *Esk* and *Express*, although the change over from conventional armament to minelayer could be, and during the war was, a fairly simple operation, *Eclipse* was not so converted and remained essentially a fleet destroyer. She was equipped for minesweeping, with the Admiralty Two-Speed Destroyer Sweep being fitted astern.

She served with the Home Fleet from 1935 to 1940 and while operating off Norway she was hit by a bomb and very seriously damaged.

On completion of extensive repairs she rejoined the Home Fleet and operated on the dangerous convoy route to Murmansk in the Soviet Union on the Russia convoys.

These convoys formed up at anchorages in Iceland and, depending on the time of year, would sail through the Barents Sea as far to the north and east as they could, until they arrived at the Russian port of Murmansk. Flanking this long route was the whole of the Norwegian seaboard and here the Germans had based a strong surface fleet, including *Tirpitz*, *Scharnhorst*, *Admiral Scheer* and *Hipper*, a destroyer flotilla and U-boats. There was also a powerful air force stationed on the northern airfields, in easy range of the convoys, consisting of long range divebombers, Junkers Ju 88's, the Stukas for close range dive-bombing and squadrons of torpedo bombers and scouting aircraft. The Royal Navy was therefore forced to provide very heavy escorting and covering forces for these convoys.

On 28th March 1942 *Eclipse* was in company with the cruiser *Trinidad* and the destroyer *Fury* as part of the escort of convoy PQ.13 in the Arctic Ocean when they were attacked by three large German destroyers. A sharp action followed in low visibility with snow flurries and the seas freezing as they hit the ships. One of the German destroyers, *Z.26* was sunk but *Trinidad* was damaged and was escorted to the Kola Inlet by the two British destroyers. *Eclipse* herself had been hit quite hard and was badly damaged for the second time in the war.

She again underwent repairs and emerged converted to an escort role with the emphasis on anti-submarine warfare. In this condition she joined the 4th Escort Group operating in the North Atlantic during 1943. Later that year she went to the Mediterranean with the 8th Flotilla and was present at the invasion of Italy and Sicily. While on screening duties on the 23rd July she and *Laforey* sank the Italian submarine *Ascianghi* off the 'Husky' beach-head.

In the autumn after the Italian surrender she was one of the destroyers despatched to the Aegean to carry supplies to the British garrisons on Leros and it was while employed on one of these missions and laden with troops that she struck a mine off Calino island and sank with heavy loss of life.

H.M.S. Folkestone

The badge is derived from the arms of the town and the first ship to carry the name in the Royal Navy was a 5th rate launched in 1704. She served until 1727 before being broken up. Another 5th rate was launched as *Folkestone* in 1740 but cannot have been a very successful vessel for she was sold a mere nine years later. No battle honours were awarded to either of these ships, nor to the three other small craft which subsequently carried the name.

The sixth *Folkestone* was a convoy escort sloop built in 1930 and it is her boat's badge which is featured here. She was built by Swan, Hunter and was launched in February of that year. Of just over 1,000 tons, she was armed with two single 4-inch guns and was capable of only 16 knots. She carried a crew of 100 officers and men.

As originally designed these craft were to combine both anti-submarine and minesweeping roles and so were shallow draught vessels but on the outbreak of war their functions were almost exclusively concerned with combating the German U-boats on the Atlantic convoy routes.

Although not designed for a front line role and therefore lacking any grace or beauty these sloops were to prove the work horses of the Royal Navy in the North Atlantic. They were hampered by the fact that they were terribly slow, and, when later in the war the new German submarines appeared, the sloops were always hard put to catch them on the surface.

Folkestone herself served for the whole war on this grim and largely unrewarding duty, plodding along at ten knots with a succession of slow convoys across the Atlantic Ocean in the face of bad weather and the wolf packs. No submarine fell victim to her depth charges during these long and wearisome months and no major action came her way. Nevertheless it was on *Folkestone*, and her equally unsung sisters, that the fate of the Battle of the Atlantic depended and with it the entire Allied war effort against Germany. It is fitting therefore that her badge should be included herewith in company with the more famous ships of the Royal Navy.

H.M.S. Galatea

In Classical mythology Galatea was a sea-nymph, the daughter of Nereus and Doris and the badge shows her adorned with a suitable crown on a blue field. The first ship to be so named dates from 1776 and was a 6th-rate. She earned the battle honour Penobscot in 1779 and was broken up in 1783.

A 5th rate launched in 1794 perpetuated the name and she added lustre to it with the battle honour Groix the following year. She was broken up in 1809 but another 5th rate was named *Galatea* in 1810 and she soon saw action at Tamatave in 1811. She was sold out of service in 1849.

The 4th and 5th ships of the name were a frigate of 1859 and a cruiser of 1887.

The sixth *Galatea* was a light cruiser of the 'Arethusa' class built by Beardmore on the Clyde and completed in 1914. She displaced 3,512 tons and carried three 6-inch and four 4-inch guns with eight 21-inch torpedo tubes. She was with the Grand Fleet, survived the war and was sold in 1921.

The seventh *Galatea* was also a light cruiser built by Scott's at Greenock and launched in August 1934. She displaced 5,220 tons and had a length of 480 feet. Her armament consisted of six 6-inch guns and eight 4-inch guns with six 21-inch torpedo tubes. She served in the Mediterranean Fleet pre-war as leader of the destroyer flotillas. She returned to the Home Fleet in 1940 and was active off Norway. In 1941 she took part in the hunt for the German battleship *Bismarck* before again being assigned in June to Admiral Cunningham's fleet based at Alexandria. Just before midnight on the 14th/15th December the German submarine *U.557* sank her with heavy loss of life.

After the war the name *Galatea* was allocated to the Humber Division of the Royal Naval Reserve in 1951 but the ninth and latest ship is one of the 'Leander' class of frigates which form the backbone of the surface navy today.

H.M.S. Glorious

Symbolised by the sunburst of her badge, the name *Glorious* has only been carried by two ships in the Royal Navy. The first of these was the French 74, *Glorieux*, which was captured at the battle of the Saintes in 1782 and would have been added to the navy had she not have foundered five months later.

The 2nd *Glorious* was one of the most unusual vessels to serve in the Navy. *Glorious*, together with *Courageous* and their half-sister *Furious*, were the special brain children of Admiral 'Jackie' Fisher.

Designated as 'large light cruisers' they were in fact as near the ideal battle-cruiser as Fisher could conceive. They had a shallow draught to enable them to operate in the Baltic and a great length of 735 feet. They displaced 18,600 tons and had turbines developing 90,000 s.h.p. which made them good for 31 knots. They had a complement of 835 and were armed with four 15-inch guns and eighteen 4-inch guns.

Glorious was not completed until January 1917 by which time Fisher had departed from the Admiralty. They took their place in the fleet with the 1st Light Cruiser Squadron and engaged German cruisers in 1917 without success.

With the Washington Naval Treaty of 1921 they were taken in hand for conversion into aircraft-carriers for which their speed made them most suitable and this took place during 1924-30. When *Glorious* emerged from this massive rebuilding she had a flight deck and an island bridge, her big guns had been replaced by anti-aircraft weapons and she could carry 48 aircraft.

She served with the Mediterranean Fleet on the outbreak of war and *Glorious* appeared off Norway in April 1940. She was on her way back to Scapa Flow accompanied only by two destroyers, when, on the 8th May, she was surprised by the powerful German battle-cruisers *Scharnhorst* and *Gneisenau*.

Only 3 officers and 35 men survived from her crew of over 1,200.

H.M.S. Gnat

Many of the ships described in this book have long and famous histories, others are recent additions which have achieved much in a few years, but it should not be forgotten that the Royal Navy has always been composed of a wide variety of vessels not all of which are remembered. Many of the smaller ships were only built for one specific operation but such is the fortune of war that they have finished up winning acclaim in very different surroundings from those for which they were built, doing tasks of which very few people would have considered them capable. As an example of these often forgotten ships of the 'back-room' navy we have selected *Gnat*.

In February 1915 Lord Fisher at the Admiralty sent for Sir Alfred Yarrow, a foremost builder of destroyers and shallow-draft vessels, and informed him that he wished to send a flotilla of special gunboats up the Danube to challenge Austro-Hungarian control of that waterway. Apart from stating that the vessels must be superior in speed and armament to the Austrian gunboats already on the river Fisher gave Yarrow a free hand with their design.

To conceal their real destination these ships were known as the Large China Gunboats and they were to be so built that they could be shipped in pieces to Salonika, sent by rail and re-erected on a tributary of the Danube in Serbia. These gunboats, of which there were to be twelve, were 250 feet long with a 36 feet beam and a draught of only four feet. They had two screws and were good for sixteen knots. They were quite well-armed for their size and mounted two 6-inch guns on their main deck with two 12-pdrs., two anti-aircraft pom-poms and six Maxims.

By the time *Gnat* was completed however the entry of Bulgaria into the war on the side of the Central Powers meant that the Serbians were outflanked and driven from the Danube and Fisher's original bold idea had to be abandoned. There was however no difficulty in finding an alternative use to which to put these craft. Mesopotamia was, in 1914, Arab territory under the influence and suzerainty of the Turks, whereas Persia was independent. The harbours on the eastern side of the Persian Gulf were Persian and therefore available to the Royal Navy whereas the towns along the river Tigris belonged to Turkey. When war was declared between Turkey and Britain in November 1914 Basra was quickly occupied by British troops and a long campaign commenced with the ultimate objective of taking Baghdad.

Thus it was that with the collapse of the Danube scheme *Gnat*, *Moth*, *Mantis* and *Tarantula* were sent instead to the Tigris to support the British advance, while four of their sisters were sent to protect the Suez Canal. They arrived in 1916. Meanwhile on land the first initial success of the army had been nullified by lack of reinforcements and was followed by the retreat to Kut and the terrible siege which followed. Despite attempts to break through the Turkish lines by the gunboats the citadel fell on April 29th 1916. It was not until nine months after this disaster that fresh British forces had been built up and were able to resume the offensive. They were aided considerably in the subsequent campaign by the supporting gunfire from the *Gnat* and her sisters, who, on one occasion, actually overtook the retreating Turkish Army and shelled its columns causing considerable panic. Baghdad was taken on March 11th 1917.

On completion of these duties *Gnat* was sent east to China and there participated in some brisk actions during the last year of the war. She was to remain on the rivers and broad estuaries of China for the whole of the 'tween war period, policing the rivers often a thousand miles inland from the sea. She was joined here by the rest of the 'insect' class and during the 1930's they were gradually being scrapped and replaced by newer vessels. However the outbreak of war halted this programme and three of the survivors, *Gnat*, *Cricket* and *Ladybird* returned after twenty years to the Middle East, joining the Mediterranean Fleet at Alexandria in 1940. Here they were soon in the thick of the fight supporting the Army of the Nile as members of the Inshore Squadron.

The initial Italian advance into Egypt, although made by an overwhelming number of men, soon ground to a halt. The reason for this was the constant fear of the Italian commander that he would outrun his supplies. Everything to keep his troops in the field had to come along the coastal road from his main supply ports of Tripoli and Benghazi. Fighting in the desert in July and August of 1940 meant that the supply of water too was of the greatest importance. Admiral Cunningham therefore had no hesitation in sending what few shallow draught warships he had to aid the army and assist in harassing the Italian divisions.

They spent long periods in company with the old monitor *Terror* pounding away at Italian gun positions, troops and supply dumps and dodging continual air attacks at their best speeds of 14 knots. They were also used to run in supplies as the army advanced and in general proved a great boon. In 1941 the advance of Rommel cut off the Tobruk garrison and the *Gnat*, under the command of Lieutenant-Commander S.R.H. Davenport, made several supply runs to the besieged port. But in October her luck finally ran out after twenty-six years when she was torpedoed by a U-boat and had her bows blown off. She was unable to steer and drifted helplessly under the very nose of the German airfields. After dark the destroyers *Jaguar* and *Griffin* found her and *Griffin* towed the little ship to Alexandria. It was planned to graft the bow of *Cricket* onto *Gnat* but this was ultimately abandoned and she saw the war out as a floating anti-aircraft battery before being broken up in 1945.

H.M.S. Grenville

The name dates from 1763 and is derived from Sir Richard Grenville (1541-1591) who commanded *Revenge* and lost his life in a gallant battle against fifty-three Spanish ships. Since 1916 it has always been carried by destroyer flotilla leaders. The original motto was *Loyal Devoir* but in 1922 the motto *Deo Patriae Amicis* (For God, Country and Friends) was transferred to *Grenville* from *Revenge* of that time. The griffin on the badge is derived from Sir Richard Grenville's crest.

The second vessel to carry the name was a flotilla leader launched from Cammell Laird's shipyard on 17th June 1916. The flotilla leader was an enlarged destroyer type designed to carry the Captain in command of a flotilla of twenty destroyers and his staff. The second *Grenville* had a displacement of 1,666 tons, was armed with four 4 inch guns and four torpedo tubes and cost £209,500. On completion she joined the Grand Fleet and was badly damaged in a collision on 9th February 1918 but was repaired.

After the First World War *Grenville* joined the 4th Flotilla, Atlantic Fleet as second-in-command and went out to the Baltic for a time during operations there in support of the Baltic States against the Communists. She remained with the 4th Flotilla until 1921 when she was paid off into reserve. Here she lay for ten years and was sold for scrap in 1931.

The name was passed on to a new flotilla leader which was laid down in 1934 and launched the following year. She was considerably longer than her predecessor, displacing 1,475 tons and she carried five 4.7 inch guns, eight torpedo tubes at a speed of 36 knots. She served as the leader of the crack 1st Destroyer Flotilla, Mediterranean Fleet during the troubled years which saw the sanctions against Italy over the Abyssinian crisis which almost developed into war, and the patrol duties off Spain during the Spanish Civil War. With the outbreak of the Second World War *Grenville* was leading her flotilla in the North Sea from their base at Harwich when, on 19th January 1940, she struck a mine and sank with the loss of four officers and 73 men. A famous picture appeared showing her bows vertically out of the water with the last man to leave clinging to her anchor just before she took her final plunge.

The following year the name was again allocated to a destroyer leader building at Swan Hunter's shipyards. She was to lead the 7th Emergency Flotilla of war-built destroyers with names beginning with the letter 'U'. It had become the policy to build the leader as part of the flotilla of eight rather than in addition to it, but the use of the names of famous seamen continued to distinguish the leader from her class, the other destroyers being named to an alphabetical system.

The fourth *Grenville* was launched on 12th October 1942 and completed the following year. She displaced 1,790 tons and mounted four 4.7 inch guns, numerous anti-aircraft bofors and oerlikon cannon and eight 21 inch torpedo tubes. She had an overall length of 362¾ feet, a beam of 35 feet 8 inches and carried a crew of over 200 officers and men. She was built by Swan Hunter's shipyard and was powered by Parsons I.R. single reduction turbines developing 40,000 s.h.p. which gave her a speed of 35 knots. As completed she carried a pleasing light tripod mast but with the increasing amount of radar and other aerials sent to sea this was later replaced by a lattice mast. She ran her trials in May 1943 and joined the fleet soon afterwards and was soon in action.

She was based on Plymouth and patrolled in the English Channel at night to intercept German convoys. On the night of the 3/4th October 1943 in company with *Ulster* of her flotilla and three 'Hunt' class destroyers, she contacted a German flotilla of five destroyers and a high-speed night action resulted off the coast of France. Both sides suffered damage and casualties but the British ships were quickly repaired whereas two of the German vessels were out of the war for six months.

Following this the whole flotilla went out to the Mediterranean where they were involved in numerous actions in the Adriatic and at Anzio in 1943-44.

In May of 1944 they all returned to Scapa Flow and underwent vigorous training in shore bombardment before being assigned to the naval forces for Operation 'Overlord', the invasion of Normandy by the Allied armies. This duty safely and satisfactorily accomplished the flotilla was refitted for tropical duties and sailed at the end of the year to join the British Pacific Fleet. This large force joined up with the huge American Task Forces for the invasion of Okinawa in 1945 and the British warships had their first taste of the 'Kamikaze' suicide attacks mounted by Japanese Naval aircraft. They survived this test and after a brief pause sailed again to mount the final softening up operations against Japan itself including shore bombardments close to Tokyo. The atomic bombs brought the war to an accelerated finish before the great invasion could be carried out and with the cancellation of Operation 'Olympic' in August 1945 the British ships returned to Australia. Here the crew of *Grenville* took part in the Victory Parade in Sydney on 31st of that month.

Grenville returned to home waters where she was put in reserve for a short time. During the early 1950's she was reduced to a frigate and her guns and torpedo tubes were landed, her upperworks were remodelled to make her a better sea boat in North Atlantic weather and extra anti-submarine equipment was installed. In this guise she continued to serve as a training ship for the next twenty years only paying off recently, as one of the oldest, and still one of the fastest, units of the Fleet. She is due to complete a refit in May 1974 for further service as a Satellite Communications ship and so will be working out of Portsmouth well after her thirtieth birthday.

H.M.S. Hermes

The name is from Greek mythology, being the messenger of the Gods, and is the same as *Mercury*. The badge thus shows him with winged helmet while the motto, *Altiora Peto* means I seek higher things and is quite appropriate. In fact the first vessel to carry the name in the service was a prize vessel, the Dutch sloop *Mercurius* of 201 tons and 14 guns, which was captured by *Sylph* off the Texel in 1796 and renamed. Despite being a popular name in the Royal Navy the name *Hermes* has frequently been associated with tragedy and the first vessel was herself lost with all hands when she foundered in a storm in 1797.

She was followed in 1798 by a small 6th rate purchased for service in the North Sea. She was of 330 tons but only survived until 1802 as a fighting craft, being sold out of service in that year. The third ship of the name also had a very brief lifespan. She was a 340 ton mercantile sloop built at Whitby in 1801 as the *Majestic*. She was purchased by the Royal Navy and renamed *Hermes* and served in the North Sea and the Channel before going out to South America. In 1809 she had been reduced to a store carrying vessel in the Mediterranean and was sold out the next year. A similar vessel followed her and also served for only a brief duration. She was a 512 ton sloop carrying 20 guns built at Portsmouth which joined the fleet in 1811. She followed the third *Hermes* by serving in the Channel and North Sea and in 1813 went out to America escorting convoys. She came to a tragic end during the attack on Fort Bowyer at Mobile in September 1814. She was disabled and went aground and had to be destroyed.

The fifth *Hermes* was another purchased vessel being formerly the merchantman *George IV* built at Blackwall in 1824. She displaced 733 tons and was a steam packet. The Admiralty bought her in 1830 and named her *Hermes* but like all her predecessors she was only a short-term addition to the strength of the fleet and was utilised as a coal hulk at Woolwich being re-named for the second time, as *Charger*. She went to the breakers at Deptford in 1854.

So far there had been no less than five ships called *Hermes* and none of them had added much lustre to the Royal Navy. The sixth however was a paddle-wheel sloop of 830 tons and mounting 6 guns. She was built at Portsmouth for colonial service in 1835. On commissioning she saw duty in the Mediterranean as a despatch boat before going out to the Indian Ocean where she took part in the second Burma War. In April 1852 she took part in the bombardment of Martaban and was present at the capture of Rangoon. After this brief period of action in a typical Victorian campaign her duties returned to the normal 'gun-boat' peacekeeping ones and she was broken up in 1864.

The name then passed on for a brief period to the old 3rd rate *Minotaur*. She was renamed *Hermes* in 1866 when already fifty years old and was assigned the job of cholera hospital at Gravesend. She in turn was scrapped at Sheerness in 1869. There was a pause of thirty years before this, as yet, far from happy name was assigned to another vessel of the Royal Navy, a protected cruiser built by Fairfield and completed in 1900. She had a length of 370 feet, a displacement of 5,600 tons and a speed of twenty knots. She carried an impressive armament for her small size, eleven 6-inch guns, nine 12-pdr. guns and two 18-inch torpedo tubes and she had a complement of 500 men.

She served on the North American and West Indies stations as a flagship for twelve years of peaceful activity. In 1913 she returned home, and, perhaps because of her name, was selected to become the depot ship for the Naval Wing of aircraft. She was converted to carry seaplanes and thus began the association of the name *Hermes* with the Fleet Air Arm. She could not however escape the associations of her name with disaster. She joined the fleet at the outbreak of the First World War in August 1914 and in October was torpedoed and sunk by the German submarine *U.27* in the Straits of Dover.

Following the first experiments with naval aviation the Fleet Air Arm (or the Royal Naval Air Service as it was then called), developed rapidly during World War I, but although the Royal Navy had many converted vessels capable of carrying seaplanes, and a few old ex-merchant vessels adapted for flying operations it was not until 1919 that the first vessel especially designed for aircraft warfare was laid down. The original name chosen for this vessel, which was to be the first real aircraft-carrier built for the job in the world, was *Mercury*. Perhaps the unhappy association of the name *Hermes* had something to do with this selection. However, when this ship was re-designed, the name *Hermes* was allocated and as such she was launched in September 1919.

Although built by Armstrongs she was finally completed at Devonport Dockyard in 1923. Of only 10,850 tons she could carry 15 aircraft. She had six 5.5 inch and three 4 inch guns for her surface protection, a speed of 25 knots and a complement of 664 excluding her air crew. She incorporated the first island superstructure to one side of her flight deck. She was described as 'a graceful little experiment' and really that is all she was but she performed a very useful role in the early years between the wars in the continuing development of naval aviation. By the outbreak of the Second World War, obviously too small and too slow for employment in the front line, she was sent out to the East Indies where her small complement of aircraft was utilised in the search for German raiders.

Due to the loss of the *Courageous* and *Glorious* early in the war the Royal Navy was faced with an acute shortage of aircraft-carriers and a more strenuous role was found for the little *Hermes* in 1940 when her aircraft were employed in attacking and disabling the Vichy battleship *Richelieu* at Dakar. She then went out again to the East Indies scouting for Armed Merchant Raiders but when the threat of Japan loomed up late in 1941 she was not attached to the newly formed force the Navy sent to Singapore, probably on account of her age and limited usefulness. Nevertheless she might remotely have helped *Prince of Wales* and *Repulse* when they were sunk by Japanese Naval aircraft off Malaya in December of that year.

She remained at Ceylon while a new fleet was hastily put together under the command of Admiral Somerville. The Royal Navy, however, was completely outclassed by the Japanese with regard to naval aviation, the Fleet Air Arm being equipped with obsolete biplanes like the Swordfish and Albacore and slow fighters like the Fulmar and Sea Hurricane. The Japanese equipped their carriers with fast modern monoplanes and had ample superiority over Somerville's ships. Thus there was little he could do when in April 1942 the Japanese Task Force which had smashed Pearl Harbour sortied into the Indian Ocean to engage him. Good fortune shielded Somerville's fleet from the striking forces of dive-bombers, torpedo-bombers and Zero fighters which the Japanese Admiral sent out after him but this good fortune did not extend to the *Hermes*. She had been sent out to the naval base of Trincomalee to pick up stores before sailing to the sanctuary of Australia but on the approach of the Japanese Naval aircraft sent to destroy that port she was sent out to sea for 'safety'. Unfortunately no fighter aircraft were sent with her and she was thus a sitting target when discovered by the Japanese airmen later the same day with her lone escort, the destroyer *Vampire*.

A heavy dive-bombing attack developed on these unfortunate ships. The Japanese later reported, "No fighters were protecting *Hermes*, nor were there any aircraft on her deck. Just before the attack, she had been overheard calling repeatedly to Trincomalee asking if fighters had been despatched". They had not and in 15 minutes the eighty Val dive-bombers led by Lieutenant-Commander Egusa had scored so many hits on *Hermes* that they had to count the few misses and deduct these for the total of bombs dropped. Riven by this unprecedented concentration *Hermes* sank with heavy loss of life. Egusa later stated that this attack was much simpler than pre-war bombing of the target ship *Settsu*.

Despite this disaster, the name *Hermes* was immediately re-allocated to the new light fleet carrier *Elephant* building at Vickers Armstrong's shipyard in Barrow. She was due to join the fleet in 1945 but after the end of the war she lay incomplete for over eight years while successive Governments vacillated on how to complete her. She finally joined the fleet in the late 1950's and incorporated all the latest post-war developments. She has now reduced to Commando Helicopter Support Ship. In this role she has had her hangar deck converted into accommodation for 500 Royal Marine Commandos and their equipment. Her only aircraft are the big Sea King helicopters and with these the commando group can quickly be ferried ashore against lightly defended targets. She relies on her escorting frigates for protection against submarines, and they would also provide light covering fire with their 4.5 inch guns. For protection against aircraft she would have to be escorted by one of the guided missile destroyers and attack by surface craft would be dealt with by a combination of all these ships as a Task Group.

H.M.S. Lowestoft

This name is taken from that of the Suffolk township and the badge shows a Lowestoft plate surmounted by an Oriental gold crown and the motto is *Point du Jour*, (Turn out early).

The first ship of the name, *Lowestoffe* as it was then, was a 5th rate built in 1697. The second *Lowestoft* was a 6th rate of 1742.

The most famous vessel to carry this name was another 6th rate launched in 1756. She was at the capture of Quebec and the victorious General Wolfe's body was brought aboard her after his last battle. After refitting in England *Lowestoft* returned to Quebec in 1760. She was lost there later that year.

A new *Lowestoft* was added to the fleet the following year. She was a 5th rate and fought at Toulon in 1759 and at Genoa the same year. *Lowestoft* also fought a notable single ship action in the Mediterranean that year against the French 5th rate *Minerve* forcing her to strike her colours and taking her as prize. Her ultimate end was a sad one for she was wrecked in 1801.

It was not until the eve of World War I that another *Lowestoft* joined the fleet. She was a 5,440 ton cruiser. She was present at the battle of Heligoland in 1914 and went out to the Mediterranean after serving at the battle of Dogger Bank in 1915. She reduced to reserve in 1929 and two years later was sold.

An escort sloop, the sixth ship to carry the name, was launched in 1934 at Devonport Dockyard. She displaced 990 tons and carried two 4.7 inch guns and a crew of 100. She served during the Second World War on convoy escort duties in the North Atlantic and the North Sea and after the war was sold and converted into the merchant ship *Miraflores*.

The present *Lowestoft* is a frigate of the 'Rothesay' class launched in 1960.

H.M.S. Royalist

The design for the badge of this ship shows the fleur-de-lis below a golden crown and the motto is *Surtout Loyal* (Loyal above all). It is therefore highly likely that the first vessel to carry the name was so called as a gesture of sympathy to the Royalists at the time of the French Revolution because the name itself was first carried in 1796. No details of the ship however are available; indeed of the eleven vessels to bear the name only the details of seven are given here.

It is known that a sloop built at Sandwich in 1807 wore the name *Royalist*. She was of 382 tons and carried eighteen guns and a most successful warship she proved to be in action. On the 1st May 1809 she captured the French privateer *Princesse*, a sixteen gun vessel, and she repeated this on the 17th November when she intercepted and took as prize another privateer, *Grand Napoleon*, an eighteen gun vessel.

During blockade duties off Southern Spain in 1813 she was prominent and on 12th October of the same year took yet another vessel when she assisted in the capture of the frigate *Weser* of forty guns. She was sold out soon after this action.

Another sloop named *Royalist* was a 231 ton vessel carrying ten guns which was launched at Portsmouth in May 1823. She served for fifteen years without seeing major action and was sold out of service in November 1838. She was replaced by the *Royalist* of 250 tons and ten guns which had been built at Bombay and purchased by the Admiralty under the name of *Mary Gordon* in 1842. She was bought on the spot especially for the campaign in Borneo against pirates and employed on this duty between 1847 and 1849. She was later converted to a survey ship in the 1850's and after seven years engaged in this useful role, was taken over by the Thames River Police and moored near Waterloo Bridge.

The seventh known ship to carry the name *Royalist* was a screw sloop of 700 tons and carrying eleven small guns. She was built at Devonport, launched in December 1861 and completed the following year for service on the American and West Indies Station. She remained there for five years and her final fate was the scrapyard at Chatham in 1875.

In 1883 a small third-class cruiser was built at Devonport and since that time the name has always been carried by light cruisers. This, the eighth *Royalist*, was a 1,420 ton ship which carried an armament of two 6 inch and ten 5 inch guns at a speed of thirteen knots. She had the typical foreign service of a mid-Victorian cruiser during the period of expansion. In 1886 she served on the Niger expedition and in early 1899 she was in the operations at Samoa. She was paid off as a receiving hulk at Haulbowline, but was still in service in 1913 when the ninth *Royalist* was laid down. She was therefore re-named *Colleen* and became a receiving ship at Queenstown during the First World War.

The next ship was a light cruiser of the famous *Arethusa* class which was completed by Beardmore in 1915. These handy vessels were in the thick of much heavy fighting and proved outstanding ships of their type, the majority, of war-time construction, following their general design. They displaced 3,512 tons and carried three 6 inch, four 4 inch and two 3 inch guns and eight 21 inch torpedo tubes. They had a length if 436 feet, a beam of 39 feet and were capable of thirty knots, with a complement of 318. The *Royalist* joined the 4th Light Cruiser Squadron of the Grand Fleet in 1915. At the battle of Jutland they were in Commodore Le Mesurier's squadron and after the main battle were stationed abreast the Second Battle Squadron during the night dispositions. At 8.45 they sighted three German battleships to the westward and turned to investigate. A quarter of an hour later they confirmed that they were enemy ships and after informing Admiral Jerram, the two light cruisers steered to attack the German dreadnoughts. The German ships turned away and contact was lost.

Royalist did see her mighty opponents again for she was present at the surrender of the High Seas Fleet two years later in 1918. They scuttled themselves the following year and the *Royalist* did not long survive them, being sold and scrapped in 1922.

The name was passed on between the wars but the next major vessel was another light cruiser, the 5,770 ton ship of the Improved Dido class which was built in 1943 by Scotts. This was the Second World War equivalent of the *Arethusa*, being handy, fast vessels equipped with good dual-purpose armament and the Dido and Improved Dido class cruisers saw the bulk of the action during the war, particularly in the Mediterranean area. *Royalist* had a main armament of eight 5.25 inch guns, with a heavy anti-aircraft battery comprising twelve 2 pdrs, twelve oerlikons as well as six 21 inch torpedo tubes. They had an overall lenght of 512 feet and were driven by four shaft geared turbines at 33 knots.

Royalist joined the Home Fleet at Scapa Flow in 1943 and saw duty in the Arctic before going to the Mediterranean in 1944 where she took part in the invasion of Southern France, supplying supporting gunfire. In 1944 she was transferred to the East Indies Fleet and en route headed a task force of escort carriers during strikes against German communications in the Aegean Sea. On reaching the Indian Ocean these same vessels carried air and sea power against the Japanese in Burma during the final drive of the army to liberate that area. She served in the post-war fleet for a period before being handed over to the Royal New Zealand Navy in 1956.

H.M.S. Sikh

The badge illustrated belonged to the first *Sikh*. She was an 'S' class destroyer built in 1918 and a sister of the *Sesame* and *Stormcloud* described earlier. She was sold in 1927.

The second and best-known *Sikh* was one of the large 'Tribal' class destroyers built just before the Second World War.

Sikh was completed in November 1938 and she was in the Red Sea at the outbreak of war and remained there escorting local convoys until December when she returned home to join the 4th Flotilla at Scapa Flow.

She served off Norway in April and May 1940 and following the evacuations from that area escorted and patrolled in the North Sea. In October she attacked a German convoy off Norway. In May 1941 under Admiral Vian, she was part of the 4th Flotilla when they attacked the German battleship *Bismark* on the night preceding her destruction on May 27th. She was based at Plymouth and took part also in Malta convoy 'Substance' in July.

The 4th Flotilla was eventually transferred to Gibraltar where *Sikh* was involved in several operations with Force 'H' before, in December, she was sent through the Mediterranean to reinforce the main fleet at Alexandria. It was during their passage that *Sikh*, *Maori*, *Legion* and the Dutch *Issac Sweers* surprised two Italian cruisers off Cape Bon and sank them both. She also took part in the two battles of Sirte when a small force under Admiral Vian fought off the main Italian battle fleet and delivered convoys into Malta.

During the course of 1942 further Malta convoys followed with the scale of air attack increasing all the time while in August she assisted in the destruction of the German submarine *U.372*. In September she was part of an ill-conceived operation against the German forces in Tobruk and it was during this fiasco that both she and her sister ship the *Zulu* were hit by Italian guns guarding the harbour and were ultimately sunk.

H.M.S. Southampton

The ship's badge is taken from the coat of arms of the city of Southampton and bears the motto, *Pro Justitia Pro Rege*, (For Justice and the King).

There have been five ships to carry this name in service, the first being a 4th-rate built in 1693. She survived until 1771 but before that time a new *Southampton* had joined the fleet. This was the 5th-rate of 1757 and she has been described as the first genuine frigate to be built in England.

The second *Southampton* was active throughout the latter part of the 18th-century, being present at the battles of Belle Isle in 1761, at the Glorious First of June in 1794, then at the Battle of Cape St. Vincent three years later when Admiral Jervis smashed the Spanish Fleet under de Cordova. This gallant vessel was finally lost when she was wrecked in 1812. She was followed by another 4th-rate which was launched eight years later.

It was almost one hundred years after the loss of the third *Southampton* that a namesake was built. This was the famous light cruiser of 1912 built on the Clyde by John Brown. She displaced 5,400 tons, was 458 feet long and carried eight single 6-inch guns and two torpedo tubes.

On December 16th 1914 during the attacks by Admiral Hipper's battle-cruisers on east coast towns it was *Southampton* who first gained a brief glimpse of the German force but foul weather enabled Hipper to get clear of a closing trap. At the Battle of the Dogger Bank in the following January the trap again closed prematurely and once more the Germans escaped.

Southampton led the 2nd Light Cruiser Squadron and was attached to Beatty's Battle-Cruiser Fleet during the opening phase of the Battle of Jutland on May 31st 1916. During the engagement between the opposing battle-cruisers Goodenough kept his four ships ahead of Sir David Beatty's ships. Thus it was that at 4.33 that afternoon while some two miles ahead of the heavy ships, they first sighted the massed ranks of the High Seas Fleet, never before seen by a British ship in wartime.

It was a dramatic moment and, true to his duties Goodenough immediately signalled: —

> 'Have sighted enemy battle fleet, bearing S.E. Enemy's course North. My position 56 degrees 34 minutes North, 6 degrees 20 minutes East.'

This was the first knowledge the British had that Scheer was out and Beatty turned north to lead him towards Jellicoe. Meanwhile, mindful of his duty to obtain the maximum information on the enemy dispositions and strength, Goodenough pressed south towards the oncoming squadrons of German battleships. He managed to take his four light cruisers to within 13,000 yards of the High Seas Fleet and was able to see the whole massed array of battleships, cruisers and destroyers which left him in no doubt that the main fleet was at last at sea. Once sure, he turned to withdraw and as he did so he was recognised by the leading German battleships who smothered *Southampton* and her consorts with 11- and 12-inch shells, any one of which was enough to destroy a light cruiser.

Fortune favoured the brave for the four ships of Goodenough's squadron escaped unscathed and followed Beatty back to the north to complete the trap. As is well known Jellicoe closed the trap but by a combination of great courage, excellent seamanship and an exaggerated fear of torpedo attack the Germans escaped not once, but twice from what should have been a decisive encounter. By the time darkness fell the British forces were between the German fleet and their bases but would not accept the risks of a night action. The initiative was therefore left to Admiral Scheer who had only one thought, how to get past the Grand Fleet to safety. Thus during the night he turned east and by luck passed astern of Jellicoe's battleships. The only forces barring his safe return were the light cruisers and destroyers stationed astern of the Grand Fleet. During the initial probes the German light cruisers *Stettin* and *Frauenlob* with others of their squadron crossed the track of Goodenough's squadron. The result was a fierce short-range action in darkness. *Southampton* and *Dublin* switched on their searchlights and opened fire. Thus they gave away their positions and were heavily hit in return. At a range of only 800 yards both cruiser forces pounded away at each other and both *Southampton* and *Dublin* were set on fire fore and aft and Goodenough's ship alone had 35 men killed and 41 wounded in a matter of minutes. *Southampton* was forced to turn away to fight her fires but not before she had scored a torpedo hit on *Frauenlob*, which sank instantly with 320 of her crew.

The German fleet eventually did break through astern of Jellicoe and never came out again until it surrendered in 1918. *Southampton* survived only to be scrapped in 1926. Ten years later the name was revived for an enlarged class of light cruisers displacing 10,000 tons and mounting twelve 6-inch guns in four triple turrets together with eight 4-inch anti-aircraft guns at a speed of 32 knots. She served in the Mediterranean pre-war and in 1939 was with the Home Fleet. During 1940 she was involved in operations off Norway and later that year was sent to Gibraltar where she picked up R.A.F. personnel to carry to Malta.

Together with the main units of Force 'H' she sailed in November escorting a convoy and was thus present at the Battle of Spartivento on the 27th of that month. She did not long survive this encounter however for on January 11th she was attacked and sunk by a force of ten Stuka dive-bombers to the east of Malta.

H.M.S. Sussex

The design of the badge is derived from the arms of the county of Sussex and features a golden martlet on a blue field. The motto is *Fortiter In Re.* The name, although carried by only four ships, is an ancient one in the Royal Navy. The first Sussex was built in 1652 and was a 4th-rate. Soon after completion she was blown up. This was during the period of the great sea battles against the Dutch when the British Generals-at-Sea and Admirals, Blake, Monck, Deane, Penn and Lawson led the ships of the Commonwealth in frequent clashes with the ships of Van Tromp, Evertsen and de Ruyter.

The second *Sussex* was put afloat as a 3rd rate in 1653 and took part in the battle of Portland when the Dutch sailed past with a great fleet of merchant ships, convinced that there was no English fleet to bar their passage. They were wrong and Blake met them fifteen miles off Portland on February 18th. The eight British vessels were opposed by Van Tromp's escorting fleet of eighty-one and the battle lasted for three days. The English lost but one ship, the *Samson,* whereas the Dutch had seventeen warships sunk or captured and over fifty of their convoy. It was a memorable victory.

Later the same year, on the 2nd June the Dutch again sailed, this time with a force of 103 warships unhampered by a convoy. In the battle that followed, known as the battle of Gabbard, a sandbank off Great Yarmouth, the Dutch were driven from the area and chased hard through the night and all through the following day before reaching the refuge of the shoals off Holland after the loss of over twenty warships. *Sussex* continued to serve until 1694 when she was wrecked..

Despite these exploits the name passed out of the service for over a hundred years and when it was revived it was for the 2nd-rate *Union,* which was re-named *Sussex* at the end of her days when she was converted to a hospital ship. She was broken up in 1816 and another century went by before the name was again revived. This time it was for a fighting ship, the name being allocated to one of the big 'County' class heavy cruisers built in the late 1920's. Because they were the first major warships built in Britain which had to conform to International Treaty limitations they were known as the 'Washington Ships'.

Britain had always depended on a large number of cruisers to patrol her long sea and trade routes and guard them in the more distant oceans against commerce raiders. The cruise of the German *Emden* in World War I had shown just how dangerous isolated raiders of this type could be against merchant shipping which was routed far from any continuous patrol and escort defence in the waters of the South Atlantic and the Indian Ocean. Therefore the Royal Navy had a very real need in the 1920's for a large number of such vessels. However because some of the larger cruisers still in service mounted 9.2-inch guns and completely outclassed any other vessels of the same type the Washington Conference imposed a limitation on the gun and tonnage sizes of cruisers with a top limit of 8-inch guns and 10,000 tons. This would not have mattered so much but in addition they limited the numbers of ships each nation could build. As no other power at that time was so dependent on seaborne supplies this was a very real blow to Britain. Because all the other nations built up to the limit imposed, the Royal Navy had to follow suit or be outclassed. But by so doing the number of cruisers available was reduced, for instead of twenty-five smaller cruisers which would have done the job required, only fifteen of the bigger ships could be produced for the same tonnage.

Faced with this problem the Admiralty came up with the best solution they could and the 'County' class was the result. They had a good endurance which made them ideal ships for distant stations and were large enough to carry out the functions of flagships on the smaller stations. In the light of developments of the time they also carried a good armament being fitted with a new pattern 8-inch gun in four twin turrets, carried on a high freeboard which afforded excellent all round fire. Their anti-aircraft potential was also good on paper with the new twin 4-inch for long-range protection. As with all heavy ships of this era the *Sussex* also carried torpedo tubes although in practice the times cruisers were called upon to use these weapons was exceedingly rare. Perhaps the most famous occasion when a 'County' used her tubes was when the *Dorsetshire* finished off the sinking *Bismarck* when the battleships of the Home Fleet had pounded her into a wreck.

Sussex herself was of 9,830 tons, had an overall length of 633 feet and a complement of 650 men. Her armament was eight 8-inch and eight 4-inch guns with eight 21-inch torpedo tubes. She was built by Hawthorn Leslie on the Tyne and was completed in 1929. In 1935 she was part of the crack 1st Cruiser Squadron with the Mediterranean Fleet under Admiral Max Horton and this squadron was brought to a high pitch of readiness when war with Italy was expected over the invasion of Abyssinia.

When the war did come four years later in 1939 *Sussex* served on the South Atlantic station during the hunt for *Graf Spee*, then in the East Indies before returning to home waters where she was with the fleet in the closing stages of the Norwegian operations in May 1940. She remained with the Home Fleet until 1943 when she went out to the East Indies, remaining with the Eastern Fleet in the Indian Ocean until 1945. She returned home and went into reserve for a time. She was not finally scrapped until 1955 when she was broken up at Dalmuir.

The name meanwhile had passed to the Sussex Division of the R.N.V.R. in 1949 and has not been revived again for a warship.

H.M.S. Thunderer

This badge is the first Official Badge and shows a hand grasping the thunderbolts of power. The motto was *Eripimus Jovi Fulmen* (We grasp the thunder of Jove). An early unofficial badge and a later official badge both depict the symbolic figure of Thor as a man with wild hair and a beard wielding a mighty hammer in the clouds surrounded by lightning flashes, but our badge is that of the mightiest *Thunderer* of them all, the great battleship of 1911.

The first vessel to be named *Thunderer* was a third rate built in 1760. She was constructed at Woolwich and was of 1,600 tons. Her major action was that fought on Lake Champlain in 1776 during October 11th and 13th. She went to the West Indies following this campaign and was lost during the great hurricane of 31st October 1780. Among her battle honours was the action against the French *Achille* in 1761 and the battle of Ushant in 1778.

Another 3rd-rate was launched as *Thunderer* in 1783. She was the most successful of them all and fought in many epic actions. She was present at the great victory of the Glorious First of June in 1794 and was at St. Lucia in 1796. *Thunderer* thundered out with telling effect in Calder's action fought in 1805 and crowned that year at Trafalgar. In 1807 she captured the French frigate *Venus* which was added to the Royal Navy. This gallant ship was finally broken up in 1814.

The next *Thunderer* was a 2nd-rate battleship launched in 1831. She went out to the Mediterranean and took part in the bombardment of Sidon and St. Jean D'Acre in the Syrian campaign of 1840. In 1863 she was utilised as a target ship to test the new armour that was to so quickly change the age-old face of British battleships and in 1869 was re-named *Comet*.

A reflection of the many diverse types of experimental battleships which followed was *Thunderer* built at Pembroke in 1872. She was described as a twin screw armour-plated turret ship and featured the new ideas of fewer bigger guns in revolving mountings instead of the old broadsides and wooden walls which had endured since the 16th century. *Thunderer* was 285 feet overall and had a displacement of 9,330 tons. She and her sister ship, *Devastation,* were a radical breakaway from the accepted ideas of their time and were the first battleships to be built without masts and yards. The armament consisted of two 35-ton muzzle loaders and two 38-ton muzzle loaders and these were the first to be fitted with hydraulic loading gear. She carried a crew of 358, was coal fired and had a top speed of 12½ knots. She had twin screws and a bunkerage of 1,600 tons giving her a radius of 4,700 miles, both features which were unique in the service. She had a very low freeboard rising only 4½ feet above the waterline and when she first put to sea grave doubts were expressed about her every feature. Despite the universal gloom which greeted her debut *Thunderer* went on to prove herself one of the most successful designs of the mid-Victorian era. She saw service in the Mediterranean Fleet before becoming guard ship at Sheerness and she was not finally sold out of service until 1909.

By this time the sixth *Thunderer* was under construction. She was the great battleship of the *Orion* class built by Thames Ironworks at Blackwall and was in fact the last British battleship to be built on the river Thames. The 'Orions' were a great step forward in battleship design and on account of their size and power were often termed 'Super-Dreadnoughts' to differentiate them from earlier *Dreadnought* types.

On a displacement of 22,500 tons they carried the new 13.5-inch gun whose heavier, 1,250-lb shell had greater penetrating power than the earlier 12-inch mounted by *Dreadnought* types. It also had the advantage of employing less muzzle velocity, which gave each gun a longer life. *Thunderer* and her sisters were also the first British battleships to mount their main armaments all on the centre line, super-imposed fore and aft. *Thunderer* carried ten 13.5-inch guns in twin turrets and a secondary armament of sixteen 4-inch guns. She was 581 feet long, had a beam of 88½ feet and a speed of 21 knots. Her complement was 738 officers and men. The cost was approximately £1,700,000 for each ship. *Thunderer* was one of the first battleships to be fitted with the Scott experimental director firing device which had the effect of increasing the range of effective firing from 9,500 yards to 14,000 yards.

On completion *Thunderer* became the flagship of Admiral Prince Louis of Battenberg, who was the Commander-in-Chief of the Blue Fleet during the manoeuvres of 1912. He it was who brought the Royal Navy to such a high state of readiness in 1914 and who was hounded out of office by an ignorant public vendetta on the outbreak of war which was directed at his German ancestry. His son, Lord Mountbatten of Burma was to vindicate his father in later years.

In 1913 *Thunderer* was the flagship of Vice-Admiral Sir John Jellicoe, soon to become the Commander of the Grand Fleet. On the outbreak of the war she served in the Second Battle Squadron and was present at Jutland. After the war *Thunderer* served as a cadets' seagoing training ship and appeared painted white in the Mediterranean at this time. It was not until 1926 that she was finally put on the sales list, long after her sisters had been broken up under the terms of the Washington Naval Treaty. Even so, like *Warspite,* she remained a fighting ship to the end and while on her way to the breaker's yard she broke her tow and ran aground off Blyth.

With her end passed the warships named *Thunderer* but the name has been kept alive during recent years when the Royal Naval Engineering College at Keyham, Plymouth was so named in 1946.

H.M.S. Tiger

One of the oldest names in the Royal Navy, *Tiger* boasts an outstanding record over four hundred years. The badge of the *Tiger* is obvious, while the motto is a proud challenge, *Quis Eripet Dentes,* Who will draw my teeth?

The first vessel was classified as a Galleass and she was built in 1546. Although it is not recorded as being broken up until 1605 it was the second *Tiger*, a hired ship, which won renown during the time of Queen Elizabeth I. She was with Drake's squadron during 1585-86 when he sailed into the Spanish West Indies and pillaged and sacked Santiago, San Domingo, Porto Praya, Cartagena and Saint Augustine. And she it was that fought the Spanish Armada when they sailed up the Channel between July 21st and 29th 1588 seeking revenge.

She was followed by the third *Tiger*, a 4th-rate, which was to add even greater lustre to an already famous name. She was launched in 1647 and served in the Royal Navy for almost one hundred years, being rebuilt no less than three times in the course of her long service. Her years with the fleet spanned the period from Cromwell and the Dutch Wars to the battle of Marbella. During this long time two other *Tigers* were added to the fleet. One was a prize, a 4th-rate taken in 1678 and sunk in defence of Sheerness the following year, while the 5th was a hired ship between 1695 and 1696.

During this century the battle honours of the third *Tiger* ring out like a trumpet call of victory, Portland, Gabbard and Scheveningen in 1653, Lowestoft, 1665, Orfordness 1666. Then came Solebay in 1672 during the Third Dutch War. Against the French, the battle of Barfleur thwarted one of many invasion threats and her final honour was that of Marbella in 1705. This famous *Tiger* was finally wrecked in 1742.

Her replacement was another 4th rate launched in 1747. She fought the French in the East Indies and added the honours Chandernagore, Sadras in 1757-8, and

Cuddalore and Negapatam in 1758 with Porto Novo in 1759 under Admiral Pocock. The sixth *Tiger* was sold in 1765, while the seventh, a 3rd rate taken as prize in 1762 served until 1783. The eighth was the former British 3rd rate *Ardent* captured by the French and re-taken at the battle of the Saintes in 1782. She was renamed *Tiger* but sold the following year.

A succession of smaller vessels followed until 1799 when a *Tiger* ship added the battle honour, Acre, and in 1801, Egypt, to the long tally.

A sloop launched in 1849 became the eleventh *Tiger* but she ran aground in 1854 and had to be destroyed by gunfire. In 1900 came the destroyer *Tiger*. She was built at John Brown's shipyards and had a length of 218 feet and a displacement of only 380 tons. She was armed with a single 12 pdr and five 6 pdrs together with two 18 inch torpedo tubes. She was rated as a 'Thirty-knotter' and during exercises on the 2nd April 1908 she was rammed and sunk by the cruiser *Berwick* with the loss of thirty six officers and men.

The largest and most powerful warship to carry the name was the great battle-cruiser constructed by John Brown just before World War One. She was to have been a repeat of *Lion*, but the Japanese battle-cruiser *Kongo* then under construction in a British shipyard showed a more sensible approach and *Tiger's* design was modified accordingly. Of 28,500 tons displacement, she was the heaviest warship built for the Royal Navy up to that time and she mounted an armament of eight 13.5 inch and twelve 6 inch guns, with a crew of 1,121. 704 feet in length overall she was capable of a speed of thirty knots.

Although not yet fully worked up, she fought at the battle of Dogger Bank on January 24th 1915 and was also present at the battle of Jutland on May 31st 1916, when, although hit several times by large shells, stayed in the battle and scored several hits on her opponents. Despite the damage she had received in this action the *Tiger* was quickly repaired and joined the fleet again ready for action. For the rest of the war she served with the Battle-Cruiser Force.

Post war she served in the Battle-Cruiser Squadron of the Atlantic Fleet between 1919 and 1922 and then became a sea-going gunnery training ship between 1924 and 1929 when she again joined the Battle-Cruiser Squadron for two years. She was cheered by the whole Atlantic Fleet on March 30th 1931 when she steamed into Devonport to pay off for the last time and she was decommissioned and sold for scrap in March 1932 under the terms of the Washington Naval Treaty.

The present *Tiger* was one of a class of light cruisers laid down during the Second World War. She was still incomplete when the war ended and due to lack of funds work on her was suspended for over ten years. When she was finally completed it was with a revised armament featuring a new pattern of rapid firing 6 inch gun, but unfortunately she only mounted four instead of the originally designed twelve. She also carried a new type 3 inch anti-aircraft gun. After several years service with the fleet in the 1960's, including the verbal battle between Premier Harold Wilson and Rhodesian Leader Ian Smith at Gibraltar, which was held on board her, she was taken in hand for refitting as a 'Helicopter Cruiser', thus losing whatever fighting value she previously had. The whole after part of the ship was rebuilt as a hangar and flight deck for Sea King helicopters and only the forward twin 6 inch and twin 3 inch guns are retained for limited defence. *Tiger* has a displacement of 9,500 tons, a length of 565 feet and a crew of 900 officers and men. Unfortunately for her proud name, she is, in her new guise, one of the most ugly and ungainly vessels in the fleet.

H.M.S. Valiant

The original spelling of the name was *Vailliant* and the badge features a fighting cock. The first ship of the name was a 3rd rate launched in 1759 which saw considerable action. She fought at Belle Isle in 1761 and was at the capture of Havana in 1762. She was engaged in both the battles of Ushant in 1778 and 1781 and also at Rodney's great victory over the French Admiral de Grasse in 1782 at the battle of the Saintes.

Nor was this the end of *Valiant's* war service, for under Lord Howe she was present at the Glorious First of June engagement in 1794 and added the honour Groix the following year. This proved to be the vessel's last major action and she was broken up in 1826 after an outstanding period of service. The second ship of the name, another 3rd rate, built in 1807, fought under Admiral Gambier and Lord Cochrane when they severely defeated a French squadron in the Basque Roads. Strangely enough she preceded her more famous ancestor to the breakers yard being disposed of in 1823.

The fifth ship named *Valiant* was one of our earliest iron clads. She was a much reduced version of the famous *Warrior*, hastily constructed and lacking most of her qualities. Due to the financial failure of her builders, Westwood, Baille and Company, *Valiant* was much delayed in building and had to be completed by Thames Ironworks. She had a displacement of 6,790 tons and was armed with two 8 inch and sixteen 7 inch guns. She was both sail and steam powered with three masts and a single funnel, but she was never good for much more than twelve knots. Almost valueless as a fighting ship by the time she was completed in 1868, being seven years building, she saw no employment with the active fleet but lay as a reserve unit in the south of Ireland for seventeen years. She was paid off in 1885 and lay for a further thirteen years at Devonport as a dismantled hulk. In 1898 she was converted as part of the *Indus* establishment and in 1915 became a storeship for Kite Balloons. In 1926 she was turned into a floating oil tank in Hamoaze where she remains a symbol of one of the most useless designs for a battleship ever put forward, but one which outlasted her many successors, including the sixth *Valiant,* which was, by contrast, one of the most successful of British battleships.

She was one of the famous 'Queen Elizabeth' class laid down just before the First World War. They were oil fuelled, a revolutionary step for capital ships then, and mounted the heaviest main armament of the time, eight 15 inch guns. She fought at the battle of Jutland with the 5th Battle Squadron with great distinction.

After the Great War she took her place in the post war fleet and served with the Atlantic Fleet between 1919 and 1924 before going out to the Mediterranean station for the years 1924 to 1929. *Valiant* was then refitted and her two funnels were trunked together and, from a distance, looked like one imposing flat sided one which gave her an appearance of strength and power. She then served in home waters until 1935, in the Mediterranean from 1935 to 1937 before paying off once more.

She was taken in hand at Devonport and over the next two years was completely rebuilt. All her superstructure was removed and the bridge rebuilt. All the old 6 inch guns were landed and replaced by a modern battery of twenty 4.5 inch dual purpose guns in twin turrets, and four pom-poms all controlled by directors. The elevation of the 15 inch guns was also increased to 30 degrees for better range. A hangar was built on for seaplanes with a launching catapult. New geared turbines and boilers were fitted and extra deck armour and bulges were fitted to her.

These massive alterations were still in hand when the Second World War commenced and work continued day and night to get her ready. In December she went to the West Indies for her trials.

She emerged in 1940 as a first-class unit with heavy anti-aircraft firepower. After service off Norway in May 1940 she went out to the Mediterranean to join her sister ships *Barham* and *Warspite* with Admiral Cunningham's main fleet based at Alexandria in Egypt. Here she saw a great deal of action, bombarding the Albanian port of Valona in December 1940, and bombarding Bardia in Libya in January 1941. During all these operations the Mediterranean Fleet was constantly attacked by aircraft from the German and Italian airforces. During these attacks the modern anti-aircraft battery of the *Valiant* coupled with her early warning radar set proved invaluable additions to the fleet and fully justified the money spent on her.

She covered many Malta Convoys and was present at the battle of Matapan in March when the Mediterranean Fleet destroyed three Italian cruisers and two destroyers without loss. She was hit by a bomb during the battle for Crete in May and in December 1941 was damaged by Italian 'human torpedos' in Alexandria harbour. She was in the Eastern Fleet in 1942 and the following year took part in the Sicilian landings in July, was at the surrender of the Italian fleet and bombarded at Salerno. She again joined the Eastern Fleet in the final years of the war, taking part in the bombardment of Japanese occupied Sabang in July 1944.

She was finally sold and broken up in 1948 after over thirty years service.

Today the name *Valiant* is worn in the fleet by one of the new nuclear-powered submarines that some people regard as the battleships of the future. She has a tonnage of 3,000 and gives her name to a class of five such vessels built between 1966 and 1971 with all-British nuclear equipment. They have a length of 282 feet, a beam of 33 feet and carry 95 officers and men. Their only armament consists of homing torpedoes. They are capable of continuous patrols at high underwater speed and can circumnavigate the globe without surfacing.

H.M.S. Wallace

The badge represents the arms of Sir William Wallace, the Scottish patriot who died in 1305. The only ship to carry this badge was the flotilla leader of 1918.

She was designed by the firm of Thornycroft as an improvement over existing ships of her type. The Admiralty was open to such suggestions and approval was given for the construction of two of them. A further order was placed by April 1917 and *Wallace* was launched in October 1918 just before the end of the First World War.

They displaced 1,760 tons and mounted an armament of five 4.7-inch guns, one 3-inch anti-aircraft gun and six 21-inch torpedoes. They had a length of 329 feet and geared turbines developing 40,000 s.h.p. gave them a speed of almost 38 knots as designed. Compared with flotilla leaders built to Admiralty designs at the same period the Thornycroft ships looked much larger on account of their high freeboard and big, flat funnels. They led the running flotillas throughout the 1920's and early 1930's. In October 1938 *Wallace* was taken in hand for a long refit which involved converting into a 'Wair' anti-aircraft escort destroyer.

This involved the removal of the entire superstructure and the fitting of two twin 4-inch mountings fore and aft, with a quadruple 2-pdr pom-pom on her quarterdeck and two quadruple .5-inch machine guns. She emerged in June 1939 as a fully war equipped vessel with an armament much more suitable for the Second World War than many of the destroyers still building, even though by this time *Wallace* was over twenty years old.

In addition to her gun armament she was later equipped with radar and extra depth charges. The resultant increase in top weights required the addition of some twenty tons of ballast, later increased to twenty-six tons.

She was thus able to serve on the dangerous East Coast convoy lanes known as 'Bomb alley' throughout the entire war, although she saw additional action during the invasion of Sicily in 1943. She was scrapped in March 1945.

H.M.S. Warspite

An outstandingly famous name in the Royal Navy, *Warspite* is credited with the largest number of battle honours of any ship. The origins of the name are not clear but the most usual conception is that it was a compound name, so typical of the Elizabethan age, meaning 'War's spite', which indicated contempt for one's enemies and was an obvious reflection of the feeling toward Spain at this time. *Dreadnought* is another example which has come down over the years in the same manner. However the ship's motto is *Belli dura despicio*, which means 'I despise the hardships of war'. There is the added complication in that the word 'spight' also was used as a colloquial name for the green woodpecker.

Thus for the greater part of her long life the sixth *Warspite* carried on her gun tampions the unofficial badge showing a woodpecker and this continued long after the official Admiralty badge, as shown here, of an Elizabethan cannon was allocated to the ship.

The first ship to carry the name *Warspite* was launched in March 1596 and displaced 650 tons, mounting a total of thirty-six guns. Her first exploit was that of the sortie mounted by the Earl of Essex against Cadiz in June of that year when her commander was Sir Walter Raleigh. Raleigh took *Warspite* under the guns of the forts guarding Cadiz harbour and closed his large opponents, burning *St. Philip* and capturing *St. Andrew*.

Warspite was present at several other victorious actions against the Spanish, including Essex's expedition to the Azores in 1597 and the destruction of the Spanish Fleet at Kinsale in 1601. The death of Elizabeth I was followed by a period of recession in the Navy. When war with France and Spain again became a reality in 1627 the only expedition mounted that summer, against La Rochelle, in which *Warspite* was one of the ships included, was a dismal failure. The ship saw no further action and after service as a harbour hulk was sold out in 1649.

The second *Warspite*, *(Warspight)*, appeared in the Royal Navy after the Restoration and the First Dutch War. Built at Blackwall on the Thames she joined the fleet in 1666. Under the command of Robert Robinson she was present at the Battle of St. James Day (25th July) and in September she distinguished herself in the capture of the French *Rubis* off Dungeness.

After a brief interval of peace a treaty between Charles and Louis XIV led to a renewal of hostilities against the Dutch and *Warspite* was present at Southwold Bay when a combined British and French fleet suffered heavy casualties and the loss of their flagship with no return. The Dutch withdrew to the Scheldt and attempts to lure them out to battle only resulted in the skirmish off Schooneveld in 1673 during which *Warspite* lost her captain. In August of the same year the British fleet fought the Battle of Texel, but again heavy fighting brought about no decisive result.

In 1689, with the support of Louis XIV, James II landed in Ireland and besieged Londonderry. *Warspite* was in the fore of battle at the Battle of Barfleur in 1692 and the decisive Battle at La Hogue the same year during which no less than twelve French ships were burnt in sight of James and his French army.

Warspite was paid off and rebuilt at Rotherhithe, re-joining the fleet in 1702. Under the command of Captain Loades *Warspite* captured the French *Hasard* in 1703. The following year she was present at the capture of Gibraltar under Rooke, and was severely damaged in the hard-fought battle of Velez Malaga. In 1709 *Warspite* took the French ship *Maure* and five years later was renamed *Edinburgh* not being finally broken up until 1771.

The third ship of the name was a 3rd-rate built in 1758, which mounted 74 guns on a displacement of 1,850 tons. At the Battle of Lagos in 1759 the British fleet under Boscawen destroyed two French vessels and captured *Modeste* and *Téméraire.*

In November *Warspite* was under Hawke's flag when at Quiberon Bay he completely destroyed the French ships there. *Warspite* served as a hospital ship between 1778 and 1783 before being renamed *Arundel* in 1800. The 4th *Warspite* was also a 74 built at Chatham in 1807.

Warspite saw service in the Baltic, the Channel and in the Mediterranean under Captain Blackwood. Later, in 1814, she took troops up the St. Lawrence to Quebec during the war with America. After Waterloo *Warspite* was rebuilt and enlarged and served all over the world, being the first battleship to circumnavigate the globe in 1826-27 under Dundas. She saw no more active service after 1846 but after being laid up for many years she was lent to the Marine Society before being burnt at Woolwich in 1876. The 2nd-rate *Conqueror* was lent by the Admiralty to replace her and renamed *Warspite* and in this guise she survived until 1918 until she too was destroyed by fire.

The next active unit of the fleet to bear the name was the armoured cruiser launched at Chatham in January 1884. *Warspite* displaced 8,400 tons, had engines which gave her a speed of seventeen knots and mounted four 9.2-inch guns and ten 6-inch guns. She served in the Pacific for four years and was then based on Queenstown. She went out to the Pacific again in 1899 but was finally sold in 1905.

The seventh *Warspite* was the best known warship of this century. She was one of the *Queen Elizabeth* class battleships and when she joined the Grand Fleet in 1915 she was the last word in battleship design. The five vessels of this class were the first Capital Ships to use oil-fuel instead of coal, and the first to mount the new 15-inch guns. Eight of these in twin turrets made her one of the most powerful warships in the world.

The 5th Battle Squadron under Evan-Thomas was actually attached to Beatty's force in May 1916 when contact was made with the German Fleet off the coast of Jutland.

When Beatty had sighted the main units of the German High Seas Fleet he led round to lure them towards Jellicoe. The 5th Battle Squadron had been engaging the German battle-cruisers but did not at first receive the signal to turn about. As *Barham*, *Malaya*, *Valiant* and *Warspite* commenced their turns to follow suit they were therefore deluged with shells from the entire fleet.

During this very hot action *Warspite* hit the German *König* several times, but in return she took at least five direct hits from heavy shells. This did not affect her fighting ability however. The 5th Battle Squadron steered to tack themselves on to the stern of the main battle line and it was at this juncture that *Warspite's* steering jammed and she performed the remarkable feat of turning alone towards the entire German Fleet. She survived this, and an attempt at torpedoing by a U-boat later, and reached Rosyth.

She rejoined the Grand Fleet but after 1916 no further opportunity for surface action presented itself. *Warspite* and her sisters continued to serve in the much reduced post-war fleet, and in the 1930's she was extensively re-built. She was thus ready for the Second World War and soon saw action.

During the German occupation of Norway and Denmark in 1940 German destroyers had carried troops to occupy Narvik in the north of Norway. It was decided that the surviving eight vessels were to be finished off before they could return to Germany and on the 13th April *Warspite* led a force of nine British destroyers into Ofotfiord. Aided by salvoes from *Warspite's* 15-inch shells all eight German destroyers were sunk as was a U-boat also found lurking close by, without loss to the British force.

Soon after this she was transferred to the Mediterranean to serve as the Flagship of Admiral Sir Andrew Cunningham based at Alexandria. On July 8th 1940 they made contact with the Italian Fleet off Calabria. *Warspite* was the only British battleship present which could reach the target and at the extreme range of 26,000 yards scored a hit on the Italian battleship *Giulio Cesare*.

In December *Warspite* and other heavy units of the fleet carried out a bombardment of the port of Valona in Albania.

In March 1941 Cunningham fought a brilliant night action off Cape Matapan and destroyed three large Italian cruisers and two destroyers in a matter of minutes with full broadsides at point-blank range.

During the evacuation of Crete *Warspite* herself was struck by a 500-lb bomb on her starboard gun batteries which caused extensive damage, killing thirty-eight men. She was repaired in the United States and did not rejoin the fleet until 1942. When she did so it was as flagship of the East Indies fleet in the Indian Ocean.

In 1943 *Warspite* returned to the Mediterranean and was present at the surrender of the Italian Fleet in September of that year. She was again heavily damaged by a glider-bomb off Salerno on the 16th of that month. She returned home and was sufficiently repaired to enable her to carry out bombardment duties with her 15-inch guns at Normandy and at Walcheren in 1944 before she finally paid off into reserve. After the war she was sold, but she ran aground on the Cornish Coast while being towed to the breakers on 23rd April 1947 and had to be broken up as she lay.

Her name has been carried on into the 1970's by the nuclear powered submarine which was completed by Vickers Armstrong in 1967.

H.M.S. Warwick

The ship was named after the Earl of Warwick and the badge design is derived from the family arms. The first ship was of 22 guns and was bought into the Navy in 1643. She was also known as the *Old Warwick* and she was broken up in 1660. There was another ship in the service with the name *Constant Warwick* which is popularly thought of as the first frigate. She was bought in 1649 and fought at the battles of Schooneveld in 1673 and Beachy Head in 1690. She was surrendered in 1691.

A 4th-rate followed in 1696 and she survived until 1726 before going to the breakers yard. Another 4th-rate succeeded her in 1733 and she was in action at the battles of Toulon in 1744, the battle honour Hispaniola was added in 1748 but she surrendered in 1756, and, although re-captured in 1761, was not re-instated into the fleet.

Yet a third 4th-rate was launched in 1767 but added no further major honours to the name *Warwick* and she was sold in 1802. For over a century the name did not feature in the Navy List. Then in 1917 a destroyer of the 'V' and 'W' class was launched from the shipyard of Harland & Wolff and she became the 5th *Warwick*. It is her boat's badge that is featured here.

She displaced 1,100 tons and carried four 4-inch guns and six 21-inch torpedo tubes at a speed of 34 knots. She was completed in March 1918 and flew the flag of Admiral Keyes during the gallant blocking operations at Zeebrugge and Ostend in that year. On her way back from the latter operation she was mined and broke her back. Escorted home, she was repaired and continued to serve for another quarter of a century.

During World War II she was on Atlantic escort duty for most of the time and in 1943 took part in patrols in the Bay of Biscay. On the 20th February she was torpedoed and sunk by the *U-413* off Trevose Head, Cornwall.

H.M.S. Wild Swan

The name dates back to 1876 when a Victorian sloop took the water. A typical product of her era she was small and slow but sufficient to show the flag in the more distant outposts of the Empire which she did without major incident for a quarter of a century. Strangely enough when 'Jackie' Fisher instituted his 'new-broom' system which meant scrapping all the old ships in the fleet which could neither fight nor run away, the *Wild Swan* survived and in 1912 was renamed *Columbine*. She served until 1920 before being discarded. Meantime the second *Wild Swan* had joined the fleet.

She was one of the Modified 'W' class destroyers laid down towards the end of World War I. These vessels were without a doubt the finest of their type when they went to sea and showed a marked advance over all foreign destroyers. They had a standard displacement of 1,112 tons and carried four single 4.7-inch guns as their main armament, with two 2-pdr pom-poms for aerial defence and two sets of triple 21-inch torpedo tubes. With a complement of 134 men they were powered by turbines developing some 27,000 s.h.p. giving them a speed of 34 knots.

Wild Swan herself was laid down at the yard of Swan Hunter in July 1918 but by the time she was launched on the 17th May the following year the war was over. However it was decided to complete eight of these ships for the post-war fleet and *Wild Swan* was completed on the 14th November 1919.

It was in 1921 that a drastic re-organisation of flotillas took place and they were reduced in size to one leader and eight destroyers only. *Wild Swan* was retained with the reduced 3rd Flotilla which remained an Atlantic Fleet unit throughout 1922 but was allocated to the Mediterranean in 1923.

No new destroyers were laid down for almost ten years after the First World War and the Modified 'W's' were the most modern ships of this type for all this period and thus were rarely out of commission. The 3rd Flotilla remained a Mediterranean

Fleet unit until 1929, under the newer leader *Keppel* from 1925. It should not be thought that this period was one of complete relaxation for although the war was over in Europe the negotiations with Turkey dragged on in a permanent state of tension lest war be resumed. This is indeed what came to pass between Greece and Turkey in 1922, ending with the sacking of Smyrna by the Turkish Army amid scenes of destruction and carnage.

The 3rd Flotilla was despatched to the Aegean with their Depot Ship *Sandhurst* to supervise the evacuation of Greeks lest they too be slaughtered. When the new destroyers of the 'A' class joined the fleet they replaced *Wild Swan* and her contemporaries in the 3rd Flotilla and for the first time in ten years they paid off into reserve.

Wild Swan remained in reserve throughout most of the thirties while the threat of war with either Italy or Germany grew larger. The accepted life-span of vessels of the destroyer type was fifteen years, so that *Wild Swan* and her sisters should have gone to the scrapyards in 1934, but during the economic crisis of the early 1930's little money was made available to build replacements and the 'V' and 'W's' remained in the reserve fleet in case they should be needed, and needed they were in September 1939 when the outbreak of war found the Royal Navy grossly under strength.

On September 3rd 1939 *Wild Swan* was completing a refit designed to make her ready for combat and, under the command of Lieutenant C. J. L. Younghusband, was to join the 18th Flotilla in the Western Approaches. Here she was to serve for the rest of the time left to her with one notable exception. With the breathtaking advance of the Germans through France and the Low Countries in May 1940 many of the available destroyers were rushed into the English Channel to land reinforcements, provide support gunfire, and ultimately evacuate the B.E.F. Such was the task allotted *Wild Swan* on 23rd May when she went to the assistance of the 20th Guards Brigade which had been taken to Boulogne to assist the 21st Infantry Division. The port was soon invested by the 2nd *Panzer* Army and the destroyers steamed up and down outside the port laying down supporting gunfire when requested, being constantly attacked by waves of Stuka dive bombers as they did so. Despite hard fighting the end was inevitable and at 17.30 that evening the evacuation of the port was authorised and the destroyers entered the port under shell and mortar fire to take the troops away.

Heavy dive-bombing and mortar fire caused some damage to the first ships to enter but they loaded up and pulled away, the first two ships taking off some 1,050 men of the Welsh Guards. *Wild Swan* and *Venomous* then went in, followed by *Venetia.* As she nosed past the harbour entrance a concentrated barrage was opened by the German artillery flanking the harbour which severely damaged the *Venetia* and she had to back out heavily on fire.

Wild Swan was already alongside and returned the fire with her main armament. German tanks were then seen clattering down the main street to the harbour and at point-blank range over open sights, *Wild Swan* scored a direct hit on the leading one; this deterred the others and must have been a unique instance in any nation's naval history of a direct combat between a destroyer and a tank. By 21.00 the destroyers had embarked another thousand men and pulled out heavily laden. *Wild Swan* grounded on the way out but managed to get clear.

They returned to Dover but *Wild Swan* was soon ordered back across the Channel again to evacuate more exhausted troops from the Dunkirk beaches. After such intensive action the subsequent return to the routine escort duties of the North Atlantic was something of an anti-climax. She continued to serve in the Western Approaches for the next two years.

The slow convoy H.G.84 was on passage from Gibraltar to England during June 1942 and consisted of twenty merchant ships with a C.A.M. Ship and a rescue ship escorted by one sloop and three corvettes under the command of Captain F. J. Walker. Against this convoy the Germans concentrated no less than a whole U-boat group, succeeding in swamping the defences and sinking five ships in one night alone. What the submarines had commenced the Germans now hoped an ace bomber group would complete and on the evening of 17th June twelve Junkers Ju.88 bombers were despatched against the convoy and its exhausted escort.

Wild Swan, which had been supplementing the escort, had earlier that day left it and was some fifty miles to the east at 22.05, when, while it was still light, she began passing through a Spanish trawler fleet busy about its peaceful business. *Wild Swan's* captain, Commander C. E. Slater, had no illusions when he sighted the twelve German bombers flying westward. He realised that they were heading for the convoy and could easily decimate it. He also knew that his old destroyer was alone and without any hope of assistance but he did not hesitate. Signalling a general warning to the convoy he opened fire against the German formation.

Provoked by this the whole German formation vented their wrath on the *Wild Swan* and the unfortunate Spanish trawlers. The result was one of the fiercest air-sea battles of the Second World War. The bombers attacked the British destroyer in waves of three. She was hit badly by the first wave, missed by the second and hit again by the third. Meanwhile no less than three of the unlucky Spanish boats had got in the way of the bombers' attacks and were blown to pieces. The bombers now returned and attacked *Wild Swan* singly as she slowly sank by the stern but in the last ten minutes of concentrated action the *Wild Swan* destroyed four of the Junkers by gunfire and so damaged another that its pilot collided with one of his companions and both plunged into the sea. Only half the squadron thus survived to return to France. Little wonder that the name is an honoured one in the Royal Navy.

Index

BIBLIOGRAPHY

Warships of World War 1 by H. M. Le Fleming. Ian Allan, 1962.

Warships of World War 2 by H. T. Lenton & J. J. Colledge. Ian Allan, 1964.

Steam at Sea by K. T. Rowland. David & Charles, 1973.

H.M.S. Warspite by Captain S. W. Roskill. Collins, 1957.

The Mighty Hood by Ernle Bradford. Hodder & Stoughton, 1959.

British Sea Power by B. B. Schofield. Batsford, 1967.

Make a Signal by Jack Broome. Putnam, 1955.

Crests and Badges of H.M. Ships by Alfred E. Wightman. Gale & Polden, 1957.

The Bismarck Episode by Russell Grenfell. Faber, 1948.

Nine Vanguards by P. K. Kemp. Hutchinson, 1948.

The War at Sea (4 Volumes) by Captain S. W. Roskill. H.M.S.O., 1954-63.

Endless Story by 'Taffrail'. Hodder & Stoughton, 1931.

British Warship Names by Captain T. D. Manning & Commander C. F. Walker. Putnam, 1959.

Alfred Yarrow by Lady Yarrow. Arnold, 1931.

The Nine Days of Dunkirk by A. D. Divine. Faber, 1959.

With the Battle Cruisers by Filson Young. Cassell, 1921.

A Sailor's Odyssey by Viscount Cunningham of Hyndhope. Hutchinson, 1951.

Flotillas by Lionel Dawson. Rich & Cowan, 1933.

British Destroyers by Edgar March. Seeley Service, 1966.

British Battleships by Dr. Oscar Parkes. Seeley Service, 1966.

Battleships of World War 1 by Antony Preston. Arms & Armour Press, 1973.

Jutland by Captain Donald MacIntyre. Evans, 1957.

The Grand Fleet 1914-16 by Viscount Jellicoe of Scapa. Cassell, 1928.

The Blunted Sword by David Divine. Hutchinson, 1964.